The New Authoritarianism

D1103148

Salvatore Babones

The New Authoritarianism

Trump, Populism, and the Tyranny of Experts

polity

First published in 2018 by Polity Press

Reprinted 2018, 2019 (four times)

Polity Press
65 Bridge Street
Cambridge CB2 1UR, UK

Polity Press
101 Station Landing
Suite 300
Medford, MA 02155, USA

ISBN-13: 978-1-5095-3308-4
ISBN-13: 978-1-5095-3309-1(pb)

A catalogue record for this book is available from the British Library.

Library of Congress Cataloging-in-Publication Data

Names: Babones, Salvatore J.
Title: The new authoritarianism : Trump, populism, and the tyranny of experts
    / Salvatore Babones.
Description: Cambridge, UK ; Medford, MA : Polity, 2018. | Includes
    bibliographical references and index.
Identifiers: LCCN 2018004119 (print) | LCCN 2018018426 (ebook) | ISBN
    9781509533114 (Epub) | ISBN 9781509533084 (hardback) | ISBN 9781509533091
    (paperback)
Subjects: LCSH: Liberalism. | Populism. | Democracy. | BISAC: SOCIAL SCIENCE
    / Sociology / General.
Classification: LCC JC574 (ebook) | LCC JC574 .B32 2018 (print) | DDC
    320.56/62--dc23
LC record available at https://lccn.loc.gov/2018004119

Typeset in 11 on 15 Sabon by
Servis Filmsetting Ltd, Stockport, Cheshire
Printed and bound in Great Britain by TJ International Ltd, Padstow

For further information on Polity, visit our website: politybooks.com

Contents

Preface

What happened? Posed as a rhetorical question, the title of Hillary Clinton's election memoir manifests the confused anguish of the global expert class over the election of Donald J. Trump to the Presidency of the United States. Had Clinton lost to Bernie Sanders or a generic "alternative" Republican, the world would not have stood still. But it did stand still for President Trump. Experts of all kinds decry his lack of qualifications, recoil at his speech and behavior, and warn of the gathering threat to the future of democracy. Trump is crass, certainly. But a threat to democracy? Trump is a populist and a boor, but he is no dictator. And his time in office has been anything but a march to crush all opposition: the Republican Congress can't decide whether to work with him or against him and a hostile judiciary routinely challenges his every order. If Trump is a dictator, he is not a very good one. Overall, his administration is probably best described as "beleaguered" rather than "tyrannical."

The closest the United States has ever come to a true populist tyranny was the Presidency of Andrew Jackson (1829–1837). The modern Democratic Party was born in the election of 1828 with Jackson at its head. The Nashville patriarch Jackson, a war hero, Indian fighter, property developer, and large-scale slave owner, won a landslide victory over the Boston patrician John Quincy Adams. The incumbent President Adams was like George W. Bush, Barack Obama, and Hillary Clinton all rolled into one: the son of a President, a Harvard professor, and a former Secretary of State. No one was more qualified to be President than he was. But Jackson had the charisma – and the votes.

Jackson portrayed himself as a man of the people, and the crowds at his inauguration really were the largest ever recorded at the time. After taking the oath of office, he rode his own horse to the White House, where he threw the doors open to the public. Once in power, he vetoed a bill that would have reauthorized the Bank of the United States (the nineteenth-century equivalent of the Federal Reserve), earning the wrath of the financial establishment. To maintain his popularity, Jackson forcibly dispossessed Native Americans, fought a proxy war with Mexico over Texas, and conspired to repress the freedom of speech of anti-slavery activists. Through such policies he won reelection with a second landslide victory in 1832.

It is hard to imagine Trump's Mar-a-Lago ever becoming a site of tourist pilgrimage like Jackson's former slave plantation, the Hermitage. Nor is it easy to imagine Trump riding a horse to work on his first day in office, even if his Secretary of the Interior did. Yet despite being labeled "King Andrew" by his opponents, Jackson respected the two-term tradition set by George Washington and did not run for the third term that he surely would have won (the Twenty-Second Amendment limiting Presidents to two terms was still more than a century in the future). The United States Constitution and system of government held firm, and Jackson's hand-picked successor, Martin Van Buren, was booted out after one term.

Jackson was vilified by the liberal "Whigs" of his day, but "Jacksonian Democracy" has come down to us as a byword for the idea that "government is controlled by the people" and "that a nation exists to serve its citizens," in the words of Donald Trump's inaugural address. Though such populist demands are often dismissed by political theorists as leading to a degenerate "majoritarian" form of democracy, ordinary people might be forgiven for assuming that the whole point of democracy is majority rule. Majority rule, the populist core of Jacksonian Democracy, does not imply any particular policy platform. It merely implies that the people be placed at the center of the political process. It is the demand of the disenfranchised that they be heeded and heard. As with Jackson, so with Trump.

Democracy is, in Abraham Lincoln's words, the government "of the people, by the people, for the people." Much repeated, Lincoln's mantra is little understood. It encapsulates, in one slogan, the strengths of three different political traditions. Government of the people, of the whole people in a single unified nation, is at the heart of conservatism. Government by the people, ensuring all people their due share in their own government, is at the heart of liberalism. And government for the people, for the benefit of the great majority of the people, is at the heart of progressivism. In balance (and in tension), conservatism, liberalism, and progressivism all contribute to the health and vitality of democracy.

Out of balance, they can destroy it. Over time, liberalism has evolved from a philosophy of individual freedoms balanced by the freedoms of others into a philosophy of individual rights that take precedence over those of the democratic polity itself. Ensuring all people the right to share in their own government is certainly a good thing, but once a privilege is defined as a "right" it slips out of the realm of democratic decision-making and into the realm of personal entitlement. As the list of such unalienable rights grows, the power to govern for the people slips out of the hands of the people and into the hands of experts, the experts who through education, social status, or sheer rhetorical agility are able to gain for themselves the authority to define those rights. The authority to identify new rights in effect gives its holders the power to define the limits of democracy itself. This authority forms the basis for the "new authoritarianism" of the book's title.

Liberalism is not some kind of problem or necessary evil. Liberalism is a good thing. But conservatism and progressivism are good things, too. The danger in today's liberalism is that many liberals no longer accept the fundamental legitimacy of these other ways of thinking about political society. Worse, liberals are apt to use their control over elite political discourse to delineate those ideas that are acceptable from those that are not. This is no idle power. Internet search providers, social networks, and even web hosting services are increasingly acceding to liberal pressure to control speech in much the same way as traditional publishers and broadcast networks have always controlled access to audiences. The freedom to speak only to yourself is no freedom at all. This is the tyranny that threatens Anglo-American democracy: the "tyranny of the expert class."

The simple fact is that Donald Trump is not the leader of a white supremacist revolution that is sweeping America. The Stormtroopers in the street are more likely to be Star Wars fans than neo-Nazis. But the only way to know that is to talk to people, not to vilify people. Blocking people on social media – or worse, demanding that internet companies censor what people can hear – is no way to go about fostering political conversation. Tolerance is what fosters conversation. For many years, tolerance was the watchword of the liberal intelligentsia, and education its default strategy. Over the last three centuries of Anglo-American history, this gently-gently approach to political change has proven remarkably successful. People in the United States, United Kingdom, and much of the rest of the world are now less racist, less sexist, less homophobic, and more liberal-minded than ever.

Today's liberals seem determined to throw away that noble record in the pursuit of an ideological authority that puts them at odds not just with national electorates, but with democracy itself. Populism, if not a positive alternative for setting politics on a new and better course, is at least a powerful force for breaking the tyranny of the expert class. It is the old antidote to the new authoritarianism. People looking for a political savior in this age of unbelief might have hoped for a more plausible paladin than Donald Trump. But there are reasons to hope that we will have a better politics after the Trump Presidency than we could ever have had without it.

* * *

I am an American academic living in Australia. That gives me both a personal stake in and a strategic distance from the tumultuous events of the Trump era. On January 20, 2017, I watched President Trump's inaugural address with the interest of a citizen and the eagerness of a social scientist. Along with everyone else, I expected to hear a speech like no other that had ever been delivered from the Capitol balcony. But the speech I heard was very different from the speech heard by the rest of the expert class. Where others detected reverberations of Hitler's Nuremberg rallies, I recognized the long-silent call of old-fashioned American populism – and I liked it. I have colleagues who marched out on January 21 to organize neighborhood self-defense associations. I sat down to write a book.

I would like to thank John O'Sullivan, CBE, for reading that first manuscript and strongly encouraging its eventual publication; Dr. James Kierstead, for his insightful advice on the further development of the book; Aija Bruvere, for reading and discussing repeated working drafts; Melinda Mitchell, for expeditiously returning draft chapters with overwhelming praise and well-targeted corrections; Chris Weston, for his valuable suggestions about the fallibility of experts; and Heather E.G. Brownlie, Esq., AICP, for her detailed comments on the text and enthusiastic support for the project as a whole.

Moving closer to the final draft, I must thank my literary agent, Peter Bernstein, for believing in me and in the book. My Polity editor, Dr. George Owers, made important intellectual contributions to the development of the manuscript, calling to mind a lost golden age of publishing in which editors were true collaborators in giving birth to great books. Two anonymous reviewers chosen by Dr. Owers provided positive and even transformative feedback that contributed to a much improved text. And Fiona Sewell provided (non-authoritarian) expert copy-editing, offering many welcome improvements to the language of the text.

Finally, I dedicate this book to Michael Falsetta in recognition of thirty years of friendship. Thanks, Mike. An expert of great authority once proclaimed that you are "worth nothing." And yet I always seem to find reasons to disagree.

Salvatore Babones
January 7, 2018

1

Freedoms, Rights, and the Liberal Ideal

Liberalism is the world's dominant political philosophy, and populism its mortal foe. At first glance it might seem like liberalism is in retreat, and nowhere more so than in its traditional bastions in the United States and United Kingdom. The arch-liberal Democratic Party Presidential candidate Hillary Clinton narrowly survived a primary challenge from the progressive populist Bernie Sanders, only to lose the election to the conservative populist Donald J. Trump. Clinton lost despite backpedaling on many of her liberal ideals as the election season progressed, including especially her commitment to free trade. Meanwhile Britain voted to exit the transnational liberal project that is the European Union, to the self-professed "shock" and "horror" of the expert class. Disaggregating the Brexit vote by social class, only the expert class – Britain's senior managers and professionals – returned a majority for staying in.

In the rest of Europe, too, liberalism seems to be under assault. Hungary's Prime Minister Viktor Orban openly advocates a new kind of "illiberal democracy," while Poland's ruling Law and Justice Party thumbs its nose at European Union criticism of its judicial reforms. The French electorate grudgingly elected the arch-Euroliberal Emmanuel Macron in a Hobson's choice election against the National Front's Marine Le Pen. The Alternative for Germany, the Freedom Party in Austria, and another Freedom Party in the Netherlands all challenge liberal worldviews. In Russia's 2016 Parliamentary elections the various liberal parties failed to win a single seat. Further afield, in Australia the conservative party called the Liberal Party replaced its populist conservative Prime Minister with an unabashedly liberal one and promptly lost 14 seats in Parliament. Among large Western countries, only Canada seems to be moving in an unambiguously liberal direction.

But look again. Anti-liberal loudmouths may be making most of the headlines, but liberal institutions continue to forge quietly ahead. With each election cycle, politics have clearly become less civil (and less liberal) than they once were, at least in the

United States. But at the same time, the scope of public life that falls under the purview of electoral politics has steadily diminished. The role of the state has expanded inexorably, but the effectiveness of governments has failed to keep pace, with the result that most actual governance is conducted by standing bureaucracies and independent agencies. The increasing complexity of society also makes politicians more dependent on expert staffs to formulate and implement "their" policies. Laws and regulations have become so complicated that ordinary citizens are cognitively incapable of grasping how their governments really work. As a result, liberals don't necessarily have to win at the polls to have the power to make policy. Often it is sufficient merely to set the rules of the policy debate.

As politics has atrophied, unelected institutions have come to control large swathes of public life, and those institutions overwhelmingly operate according to liberal rules. For example, the independence of courts from political control, once widely considered a threat to democracy, is now almost universally accepted as a bedrock principle of good governance. In the case of Poland, the European Commission (the executive arm of the European Union) has gone so far as to declare majority political control over the court system a violation of the rule of law. They may be unaware that most US states still elect their supreme court justices. In the economic sphere, independent central banks directly control interest and exchange rates, indirectly control inflation and unemployment rates, and usually have the discretion to bail out banks (or let them collapse), intervene in markets (or let them fall), and rescue big depositors (or let them lose their savings). In theory they are even able to bring down governments by refusing to finance government debt.

Education, too, is a liberal preserve. Elected leaders may hold the ultimate responsibility for funding schools, but they have little say over what is taught in the classroom. Parents have even less influence. Textbooks are written (and vetted) by academics and school curricula have passed from the oversight of local school boards to state and national committees of educators. As a result, old-fashioned civic ideals of patriotic education have long since given way to a liberal agenda focused on multiculturalism, the celebration of diversity, and sensitivity training. The teaching of "Western civilization" has come to be stigmatized as code for institutionalized sexism and racism. And the mantra that all children should be university-ready has decimated technical education and apprenticeships in favor of liberal indoctrination at all levels. The curricula of state-run schools are heavily influenced by the admissions policies of independent universities that receive much of their funding from taxpayers but are shielded from political oversight.

In areas like medical research, disaster relief, international aid, refugee policy, the arts, and (in Europe) public broadcasting, the liberal agenda demands that the state provide resources while eschewing any role in day-to-day decision-making. The idea that public bodies like medical research councils and disaster relief agencies should be free from political interference has become so deeply rooted as to seem self-evident. But as these kinds of organizations, along with more powerful organizations like central banks and courts – not to mention the intelligence agencies – become depoliticized, they slip out of the realm of democratic governance and become the private preserve of the expert communities that grow up around them. Liberals have run roughshod over conservative and progressive sensibilities by successfully claiming that whole domains of public life are not open to legitimate policy debate. Even Donald Trump has not dared to challenge the independence of the Federal Reserve Board or the Supreme Court – at least not yet.

Populists of the alt-right, alt-left, and alt-anything,

Donald Trump included, have summoned the courage (or perhaps more accurately: the shamelessness) to question such seemingly unchallengeable liberal truths. They have demanded that entire realms of public policy be brought back into democratic politics. Their demands range from the economically unorthodox to the scientifically ignorant, from the implicitly discriminatory to the openly racist. But the principle of one person, one vote requires that their demands be heard. The populist revolt made Bernie Sanders a serious contender for the Presidency and actually brought Donald Trump to the White House. Whether Trump and his supporters will be able to translate electoral success into policy action remains to be seen, and populists in general have a poor historical track record of realizing their programs. But one thing is certain: Americans suddenly care about politics in ways that they haven't for decades. Populism may be bad for policy, but it is good for democracy.

A liberal authoritarianism

If liberal principles seem threatened, it is only because they have been so successful. Look more carefully at American, British, or European Union politics, and it is hard to find any viable alternatives to liberalism even in its supposed moment of peril. Donald Trump spews forth an endless stream of illiberal invective, but even as a President of the United States holding majorities in both houses of Congress he has been unwilling or unable to roll back the liberal agenda in any meaningful way. Liberalism is, after all, based on the idea that individual liberty is the highest political virtue – and who doesn't love liberty? "We hold these truths to be self-evident, that all men are created equal, that they are endowed by their Creator with certain unalienable Rights, that among these are Life, Liberty, and the pursuit of Happiness." These were the words that created the United States of America, and ultimately the global liberal order. Once there was any place in the world where people were free, the tyrannies of all other places became untenable. It was only a matter of time.

But over time the kinds of liberties demanded by liberals have evolved and expanded. They have shifted from a historical focus on "negative" freedoms toward a contemporary focus on "positive" rights. The philosophical construction of the concept of liberty is contentious and convoluted, but there is an obvious and intuitive difference between the simple freedoms enshrined in the First Amendment to the US Constitution (freedom of religion, speech, assembly, and the press) and the expansive rights promised by Article 25 of the UN Declaration of Human Rights (rights to food, clothing, housing, medical care, social services, unemployment insurance, and social security). Political philosophers may be able to derive one from the other, but ordinary people will understand that there is a basic qualitative difference, even if the line between the two is not always as clear as a polemicist might prefer. Nothing in philosophy is ever simple, but simply put, the freedom to pursue happiness is something very different from the right to be happy.

Political liberalism has evolved over nearly three centuries from a philosophy of safeguarding freedoms into a philosophy of demanding rights. There have been good reasons for this shift. Liberals have come to realize that freedoms on their own are not always sustainable. People sometimes vote to relinquish their freedoms. Very often people use their freedoms to enslave others. Freedom may be just as likely to be used irresponsibly as it is to be used responsibly. Thus the mainstream of liberal opinion has come to the view that the protection of basic human rights, especially the protection of minority rights, is an indispensable prerequisite for the maintenance of individual freedom. To some extent this is true. But the principle that some human rights must be ensured prompts the question of which ones. Someone has to decide, and if that decision preempts democratic decision-making, then clearly the decision cannot be left up to the people. In fact, among liberal political scientists the whole idea that the people should define the scope of basic human rights is now sneeringly referred to as "majoritarian" democracy, qualified as if it were no kind of democracy at all.

Mainstream liberals have reasoned, perhaps correctly, that the delineation of the set of human rights that are necessary for the maintenance of individual freedom can only be properly performed by experts. Those experts, the experts in human rights, are by definition educated professionals like academics, lawyers, judges, journalists, civil servants, social workers, medical doctors, and lobbyists. By virtue of dedicated study and professional practice they have made themselves the legitimate authorities on the subject. And they truly are the legitimate authorities on the subject. When you want an authority on chemistry, you consult a chemist. When you want an authority on human rights, you consult a human rights lawyer.

The problem is that politics is a unique field of human activity. Authoritarianism in chemistry may be unproblematic, even desirable. Authoritarianism in politics is dangerous, even when the authorities themselves are above reproach. In the contemporary liberal worldview, certain policies are mandatory, others are beyond the pale, and only the experts can tell which is which. Liberal democracy thus requires the obedience of the voters (or at least the citizens) to expert authority. The people are the passive recipients of those rights the experts deem them to possess. As the domain of rights expands, experts end up making more and more of the decisions – or at least of the decisions that matter – in an ever-increasing number of the most important aspects of public life: economic policy, criminal justice, what's taught in schools, who's allowed to enter the country, what diseases will be cured, even (in many cases) who will have the opportunity to run for elective office. In these areas and more, experts arrogate to themselves the authority to adjudicate competing claims for public resources and private benefits. As society evolves, the areas reserved to expert adjudication seem only to expand. In the course of normal politics, previously depoliticized policy domains rarely return to the realm of democratic determination.

The new authoritarianism of the twenty-first century has nothing to do with the Presidency of Donald J. Trump. It is neither a right-wing authoritarianism, nor a nationalist authoritarianism, nor even a conservative authoritarianism. The new authoritarianism of the twenty-first century is, paradoxically, a liberal authoritarianism. It is a tyranny of experts.

The habit of obedience

Authoritarianism has always been a dirty word. Liberal political pundits have a habit of labeling any political movement they don't like as authoritarian, if not also fascist, communist, totalitarian, or worst of all: populist. The problem with this is that although all of these things may be bad (in varying degrees), they are not the same bad thing, nor do they always coalesce in the same political movements. The Nazis may have come closest to ticking all five boxes. But that doesn't mean that all populists are authoritarians or that all authoritarians are Nazis in the making. Authoritarian governments existed long before the Nazis, fought against the Nazis, and survive in many forms today.

Authoritarianism simply means governance legitimated by demands for deference to authority. The source of that authority can be a confluence of church, monarchy, and the military, as it was in Franco's Spain, or the Leninist demand for deference to a single ruling party, as it was in the Soviet Union and still is in the People's Republic of China. The source of authority can even be a single, charismatic person at the head of an organized political movement, as it was in Hitler's Germany. The common thread running through these and the many other authoritarian systems that have existed throughout history is the common principle that people should not think for themselves. In an authoritarian system, obedience to authority is the highest political virtue.

The word "authoritarian" began its career in nineteenth-century America as a derogatory term applied to a teaching style in which the teacher posed as the unquestionable fount of all knowledge. It was contrasted with the more open, child-centered learning styles advocated by philosophers like Jean-Jacques Rousseau, Henry David Thoreau, and later John Dewey. These reformers emphasized the role of individual exploration in learning. When students are free to explore, they pursue many dead ends, but they learn as they pursue. This approach to education emphasizes the process over the outcome, the journey over the destination. Students develop their minds by asking their own questions and arriving at their own answers.

In contemporary Western educational systems, this old touchstone of "independent thinking" has been replaced by the new stock term "critical thinking skills." This is not a mere matter of management-speak. When students think independently, they reason their way toward individual solutions. Those solutions may be wrong, as the independent thinker often is. Societies of amateurs are full of opinionated ignoramuses. But vibrant democracies depend on an overabundance of opinionated ignoramuses, conspiracy theorists, quacks, know-nothings, and other loudmouths. Free thinkers will think what they want. Isaac Newton spent more time on alchemy and the occult than he did on the theory of gravity.

Though it may pain teachers to hear it, critical thinking skills teach the habit of obedience, not because teachers value obedience, but because of the very criteria on which success in critical thinking must be judged. Critical thinking teaches students to reason toward the correct answer. But what if there is no correct answer? Or what if there is a correct answer, but it is impossible to know what it is? Most public policy questions fall into these two open categories. In such cases, independent thinking won't necessarily lead people to the right answers. What independent thinking does is give the thinker – in this case, the citizen – a stake in the answer.

For example, consider the question of whether the United States should have intervened earlier in World War I. If it had, millions of lives might have been saved, Russia might not have fallen to the Bolsheviks, and Germany might have been more comprehensively defeated, changing German attitudes and preventing the rise of Nazism and the coming of World War II. Or perhaps the twentieth century would have turned out even more hor-rifically than it did. We will never know. But we do know that the delay in America's entry into World War I left time for the issue to be comprehensively discussed, for ordinary Americans to form opinions for and against getting involved, and for them to express those opinions, whatever their merits. As a result, when the United States did go to war in 1917 it was with the full support of the American people. Those who were initially against intervention, who may even have voted for Woodrow Wilson on the basis of his isolationist slogans ("America first" and "He kept us out of war"), patriotically joined in the cause.

Contrast that process with the politics behind

America's more recent wars waged in Southeast Asia and the Middle East, hatched by cabals of experts with little genuine public debate. Despite their (current) unpopularity, it is impossible to say for sure whether these wars were right or wrong, successful or unsuccessful, because the relevant counterfactuals will never be known. What we do know is that there was no consensus among ordinary citizens about America's participation in these wars. For all we know, free-thinking citizens might have made even worse decisions. History is littered with the stories of democratic countries going to war for all the wrong reasons, from Athens' gratuitous invasion of Sicily in 415 BC to America's avaricious war on Spain in 1898. Independent thinkers are not necessarily better thinkers. But they take responsibility for their decisions in a way that obedient subjects do not. Independent thinking is more important for the health of democracy than is the success or failure of any particular policy decision.

Discretionary wars brightly illustrate the rise of the new authoritarianism because they crystalize decision-making processes into discrete, well-known events. But for the quality of democracy itself, the most important policy questions are those about freedoms and rights: who has them, who can grant them, and who can take them away. These are fundamentally questions about sovereignty and where it is located. The traditional American answer is that sovereignty resides in "We the People." The traditional French answer is the state, and the traditional British answer is characteristically something in between: Parliament. But these traditional answers are now being challenged. Experts increasingly assert the existence of universal human rights that are beyond the political power of the people or the state to regulate. Whereas universal freedoms may be "self-evident" (and reserved rather than granted), universal rights must be granted by someone. Under the new authoritarianism, that someone is the expert class.

The sovereignty of experts

Rights are granted; freedoms are reserved. But by whom, and to whom? In the United States the answer is clear: sovereignty resides in the people. The US Declaration of Independence is explicit on this point: governments derive their just powers from the consent of the governed. The people may grant to the government the right to exercise certain powers, and the people may reserve to themselves whatever freedoms they choose. The people can't grant rights to themselves, because a right implies an obligation on someone else to provide the service that is guaranteed by that right. When the people grant a right to the government (for example, the right to tax the people) they implicitly place an obligation on themselves to fulfill it. Similarly, the government can't grant freedoms to the people. They're not the government's to grant.

That's in the United States. In continental Europe, and especially in France, sovereignty has historically been understood to reside in the state. Though the French Constitution of 1958 nominally vests sovereignty in the people, it was born of a military coup d'état (as were many previous French Constitutions). The German Basic Law has never received a popular vote, and in fact was rejected by the Bavarian legislature, the Landtag. The Basic Law went into effect anyway, while the country was under foreign occupation, and remains in effect today. In the continental European political tradition the state is sovereign. The state grants rights to the people and the state can take them away. A state can't really grant a freedom; it can only forbear exercising its right to govern in a particular area. Thus the European Union's vaunted Four Freedoms aren't really freedoms at all. They are rights that the

EU has granted to people and (more importantly) corporations, rights that are enforceable against the European Union's constituent member states.

The EU's four fundamental rights are that (1) European corporations have the right to sell their goods in any country of the Union, (2) European workers have the right to work in any country of the Union, (3) European corporations have the right to provide their services in any country of the Union, and (4) Europeans have the right to invest their money in any country of the Union. The receiving country must accommodate these rights. This is hardly an inspiring enumeration of rights. Articles 9, 10, and 11 of the European Convention on Human Rights do guarantee Europeans the freedom of religion, speech, and assembly, but all of these guarantees are subject to regulation by the state and all of them can be limited by the need to protect the rights of others. Although in substance they promise freedoms, in form they grant rights. In Europe a speaker can be legally prevented from shouting down a competitor. That may be very civil, but it reflects regulated speech, not freedom of speech.

The United Kingdom has an idiosyncratic constitution that vests sovereignty in "the Crown in Parliament under God." But these days the Queen only says what she's told to say and God never speaks at all, leaving Parliament to run the show. The 1689 English Bill of Rights was in effect a grant of rights by Parliament to itself, and as such it can be (and has been) overturned by subsequent Parliaments. In legal form the United Kingdom isn't so much a country as a legislature. Only tradition and responsibility force Parliament to rule in the interest of the country as a whole. Not for nothing is the Conservative Party called the natural party of government in the United Kingdom. Absent a Burkeian commitment to the continuity of the political community, the UK could very well descend into chaos.

The three major Western traditions of sovereignty (American, French, and English) are very different, but in extremis they all defer to the will of the people. This deference is notionally direct in America, electoral in France, and customary in England, but it is deference all the same. Abraham Lincoln's Gettysburg Address principle of government "of the people, by the people, for the people" is enshrined in Article 2 of the French Constitution. No Western politician of any tradition can afford to be caught on camera saying that the will of the people is irrelevant (even if many behave as if it is). European constitutional traditions do not accord the same formal primacy to individual freedoms that the American one does, but they are nonetheless responsive to people's demands and desires. A French or British government that trampled on individual freedoms would not be long for this world.

The three traditional forms of sovereignty have now been joined by a fourth: the sovereignty of experts. The sovereignty of experts is a natural outgrowth of the construction of individual liberties as rights instead of as freedoms. This has occurred even in the United States, where eighteenth-century freedoms have been overwhelmed by the more recent preponderance of rights. In the United Kingdom, common law freedoms have been creepingly superseded by civil law rights. And in Central and Eastern Europe, where democratic roots are much shallower, contemporary rights discourses are often the only discourses available. The result has been a subtle shift from the power of the people to the empowerment of the people. The first is organic. The second is a discretionary grant of government.

Empowerment in itself is not a bad thing, but it is not as good as having power in the first place. When experts rule that rights must be granted to people, it is the experts who decide what rights, in what degree, to what people. Unlike governments, those experts are not directly accountable to the people and need not face the judgment of the people at election time. And they don't feel obliged to take the popular will into account – at all. Quite the contrary. Most of the expert class views its insulation from public opinion (life appointments for judges, tenure for academics, admission to the bar for lawyers, and even insulation from shareholder activists for corporate boards and CEOs) as a virtue. It is that very insulation that allows them to determine the rights of others in an objective, professional manner. Experts only have to answer to other experts. They are self-referential authorities.

This sovereignty of experts has no basis in constitutional law. But it is a reality in practice, and increasingly so. Deference to authority is particularly strong in the field of human rights, where the well-informed and well-articulated opinions of scholars count for much more than the naive opinions of ordinary people. When it comes to the creation of new human rights, the opinion of one expert may outweigh the opinions of millions of ordinary citizens. The principle of one person, one vote simply does not apply. Most experts would argue that it should not apply.

That may be correct, but it is hardly democratic. The principle that experts should adjudicate rights without regard for the popular will is a form of authoritarianism: it is governance legitimated by demands for deference to authority, in this case the authority of experts. It is only the high self-regard of experts that places them above traditional founts of authority like the church and the military. Self-regard is the key. Experts cannot be authoritative unless they speak with one voice, since differences of opinion among experts undermine their claims to exclusive knowledge. They must thus elevate their own credentialing procedures above the possibility of non-expert review and intervention. They must also be self-reproducing, selecting and grooming their own future members. In this they very much resemble Leninist party organizations. Loyalty to the profession – like loyalty to the party – is the sine qua non of membership.

It would be sensationalist (maybe even populist) to claim that a self-appointed and self-perpetuating human rights aristocracy is running roughshod over Western democracy. But with less hyperbole there has been in the West a slow but comprehensive historical evolution from the broad consensus that governments derive their legitimacy from the people via democratic mandates to an emerging view that governments derive their legitimacy by governing in ways that have been endorsed by expert authorities. The fact that those authorities are (at least for now) motivated by the desire to realize liberal ideals may be admirable, but that doesn't make it any less ironic.

Lacking an American-style First Amendment or English-style common law liberties, the European Union is especially susceptible to this new liberal authoritarianism. The EU's foundation in French state-centered traditions and its multi-tiered structure reinforce the insulation of so-called Eurocrats from effective democratic accountability. Nonetheless, the new authoritarianism also has a strong presence in other Western democracies, even in the United States. The US is a particularly important case because of its unique position in setting the policy agenda for the entire world. The extent to which liberal authoritarianism has undermined the foundations of the very democracies it claims to serve is still unclear, but if it compromises American democracy, it threatens the viability of democracy itself. American democracy must be saved from the new authoritarianism of the expert class, and the unlikely hero in this epic might very well turn out to be President Donald J. Trump.

2

The Rise of the New Authoritarians

Liberalism is not intrinsically bad for democracy. In fact, throughout most of modern history, liberals have been a force for greater democracy. Democratic reforms like the right of universal suffrage, the right to a secret ballot, and the right to directly elect one's own representatives were all promoted by liberals. But more recent liberal extensions of democratic rights have gone far beyond basic rights that are necessary to protect people's freedom of choice. For example, liberal pressure on parties to nominate a minimum number of female candidates or for states to set aside seats for members of underrepresented groups restrict rather than safeguard people's freedom to choose their own leaders. In 2016 many American liberals went one step further in their prioritization of liberal ideals over democratic freedoms. They suggested that members of the US Electoral College should exercise their nominal Constitutional right to refuse to cast their Presidential ballots for Donald Trump. With this suggestion liberals directly challenged the very logic of democracy itself.

Democracy means many things to many people, but at its core must always be the idea that the people rule the polity, not the other way around. In small polities like ancient Athens the people have ruled directly while in large democracies like the United States they have ruled through representatives. What unites the two kinds of democracy is the self-conscious sense that power ultimately rests with the people. Like ancient Athens, the early United States can justly be criticized for not admitting women and slaves to the franchise, but that is to intentionally miss the point. Looking back on history, some may claim that the United States was not a democracy until 1870 (the Fifteenth Amendment), 1920 (the Nineteenth Amendment), or 1965 (the Voting Rights Act), but from its foundation in 1776 everyone at the time could see that the United States was a democracy while countries like England, France, Spain, Austria, Russia, Thailand, China, and Japan were not. The liberal expansion of voting rights consistently strengthened American democracy, and over time many of those other countries became democracies themselves.

The right to vote is the fundamental right of democracy, and the expansion of voting rights is one of the greatest accomplishments of the spread of liberalism. Liberalism stands for the expansion of rights of all kinds, and in democratic countries liberals have consistently fought to expand voting rights, but that doesn't mean that liberals always support democracy as such. Notoriously, the federalist framers of the US Constitution did not want the President of the United States to be democratically elected. Elections to the House of Representatives have always been by popular vote, and the Seventeenth Amendment to the Constitution (1913) mandated the direct election of Senators, but the President was and still is chosen by an Electoral College. Though the Constitution is silent on how the states should choose their Electors, Alexander Hamilton argued vehemently in the *Federalist No. 68* that the President should be chosen "by men most capable of analyzing the qualities" of the candidates, men who are "most likely to possess the information and discernment requisite to such complicated investigations," so that "the office of President will never fall to the lot of any man who is not in an eminent degree endowed with the requisite qualifications."

Hamilton was quite explicit about his concern that "low intrigue, and the little arts of popularity, may alone suffice to elevate a man to the first honors" and advocated the Electoral College precisely to prevent this. There is nothing inherently contradictory in the idea of a democratic country having a head of state who is not democratically elected. Article I of the US Constitution focuses on Congress, not the Presidency, and it is clear that for the Founders the directly elected Congress was the key institution of democratic accountability, not the collegially selected President. Contemporary American liberals, for whom Hamilton is now the favorite founding father, seized on Hamilton's reasoning in *Federalist No. 68* to advocate that the Electoral College should exercise its Constitutional discretion to select a different candidate. This was liberalism at its purest but most dangerous: an explicit effort to reverse a popular decision masked by a scrupulous commitment to the technicalities of the rule of law. The liberals who advocated Electoral College independence in 2016 also had a democratic argument on their side, since more Americans actually voted for Hillary Clinton than for Donald Trump. The irony of using the fulfillment of the popular will as a pretext for subverting democracy seemed lost on them.

Liberals can live comfortably either inside or outside democracies, as the history of continental European liberalism and the reality of contemporary Third World liberalism demonstrate. French liberals turned to Napoleon III, Rwandan liberals to Paul Kagame to push forward liberal rights. In the democratic United States, one of those liberal rights is the right to vote, though American liberals have always found it difficult to win elections – at least, when they have run as liberals. Hamilton's own Federalist Party, America's first political party, disintegrated after losing the election of 1816, its fifth consecutive loss. After that the United States had no predominantly liberal party until the Democratic Party leadership was captured by liberals during the civil rights battles of the 1960s. The resulting alliance of convenience among liberals, progressives, Northern union bosses, and Dixiecrat Southern sectionalists generated the linguistic confusion that continues to plague American use of the term to this day. Although in America the word "liberal" has come to be applied to progressive, pro-poor social policies, that is neither its etymological nor its historical meaning.

Franklin Delano Roosevelt was personally responsible for the linguistic shift, characterizing his policies as "liberal" when they were anything but.

Roosevelt wrote in the introduction to his public papers of 1938 (published in 1941) that liberals believe it is "the duty of government ... to meet new social problems with new social controls," in contrast to conservatives, who believe in "individual initiative." The idea that "social controls" should be used to effect progressive outcomes was not the invention of a new form of liberalism. It was an upending of language itself. Roosevelt was an effective leader and a great President, but he was certainly no liberal. Roosevelt's linguistic legerdemain notwithstanding, the Democratic Party did not become the home of America's living, breathing liberals until they were driven out of the Republican Party of McCarthy, Goldwater, and Nixon after World War II.

Liberalism and the courts

The roots of American liberalism actually predate the Republic. Liberalism was in a sense the seminal political tradition of Anglo-American democracy. In 1649 the English people beheaded their king, then couldn't figure out what to do with their audaciously won freedom. Eleven years later England's exhausted republicans invited the late king's son to return home to restore the monarchy, subject to Parliamentary oversight. At that moment modern liberalism was born. Liberalism was and is an ideology of the dignity of the individual in the face of absolute power. In its English origins that power was monarchical, and liberalism became the house philosophy of the Parliamentary supremacists who opposed or sought to place limits on the power of the Crown. Many eighteenth-century English liberals even supported the American Revolution as a rebellion of free Englishmen against an oppressive king. During the English Civil War, Massachusetts had sent troops to fight in the Parliamentary armies against the Crown. In the 1770s, many English liberals returned the favor.

Liberalism was originally grounded in English nonconformist Protestantism. The nonconformists were those independent Protestants who did not accept the authority of the established Church of England, the church with the monarch at its head. Nonconformists stressed (and continue to stress) individuals' responsibility for their own relationships with God. Everyone (or at least every man) was expected to read the Bible for himself, which meant that everyone had to be taught how to read. In 1642, Massachusetts, that most nonconformist of colonies, became the first place in the world to mandate universal (white, male) public education. The only Federalist Party candidate ever elected President of the United States, John Adams, wrote its state constitution. He gave Harvard University its own chapter, reaffirming its independence and specifically guaranteeing the sanctity of its endowment "forever."

In England's old-established political culture, the traditional sources of authority were the Crown, the church, and the aristocracy. English liberalism was founded on opposition to these sources of authority, and liberals were the architects of England's 1689 Bill of Rights. A century later America's liberal Federalists were the new country's "in" crowd, the party of George Washington, New York financiers, Boston merchants, and Harvard intellectuals. Sitting at the top of the new national hierarchy, America's first liberals vehemently opposed the adoption of a Bill of Rights that might limit the powers of the new federal government. In the First Amendment of the Bill of Rights the people reserved to themselves the freedoms of religion, speech, assembly, and the press, and in the Second, Third, and Fourth Amendments they reserved additional freedoms. The Federalists saw no reason why these freedoms should be reserved, arguing that since the Constitution did not explicitly grant the government the right to limit them, they did not have to be protected.

The United States government has since done much that the Constitution did not explicitly authorize it to do, but those first four amendments to the Constitution have stood firm. In the absence of a monarch, an official church, or a hereditary aristocracy, the only authoritative institution in the new American republic was the Constitution itself. Early American liberals set themselves up as its interpreter, and even today the *Federalist Papers* written by Alexander Hamilton, James Madison, and John Jay are routinely referenced by the Supreme Court. The contemporary *Anti-Federalist Papers*, which argued for the adoption of the Bill of Rights to limit the powers of the new federal government, are rarely cited.

The first four Chief Justices of the United States Supreme Court were all members of the Federalist Party, giving the party control of the court until 1835, thirty years after its last serving President and twenty years after its electoral collapse. They established the doctrines of judicial review (the principle that the courts have the authority to adjudicate the constitutionality of Acts of Congress and orders of the President) and judicial supremacy (the principle that in the interpretation of the law the courts have supreme authority over the other branches of government). Judicial review and judicial supremacy are now so well established in the United States that their logic is usually taken for granted, but there are no equivalent doctrines in English common law. In the United Kingdom, historically, Parliament was sovereign. In the United States, judicial review and judicial supremacy imply that the Supreme Court is sovereign. It set itself up two centuries ago as the final authority on American law, and it has been a bastion of expert authority ever since.

Thus what American liberals have not been able to win at the ballot box, they have often sought to accomplish via the courts. Abortion rights and gay marriage came via the courts, but also the overturning of progressive policies like the first income tax (until progressives pushed through the Sixteenth Amendment in 1913) and the first federal minimum wage law. From the perspective of the twenty-first century it is hard to remember that in a previous century liberals bitterly opposed the income tax and the minimum wage, but they did. These progressive policies were perceived to infringe on the right to property and the right to make contracts. They only came to be embraced by liberals in the middle of the twentieth century, when American liberals moved out of alliance with conservative Republicans and into alliance with progressive Democrats.

The one constant in liberal politics throughout the history of the United States has been their preference for the courts over the other branches of government. You never know who might be elected President, but the courts are always run by experts. British liberals, lacking a Supreme Court to overrule the politicians, had to fight things out in the rough and tumble of Parliamentary politics – where they usually lost. The United Kingdom only established a Supreme Court in 2005 (becoming operational in 2009) under the New Labour government of the arch-liberal Tony Blair. For the previous six centuries, the final legal authority in the United Kingdom had been located in the House of Lords. The European Union, by contrast, has from its origins been an experts-only zone, formally controlled by its member states but insulated to the maximum extent possible from democratic political interference. Much more than the US or the UK, it provides the ideal institutional environment for the flourishing of the liberal authoritarianism of the transnational expert class.

The liberal coalition

American federalist liberalism may have been born with the Republic, but from roughly 1820 to 1960 liberals had no exclusive party home in American politics. The natural electoral constituency for liberalism is in fact quite limited. The core constituency for liberal politics is the expert class, the professionals and managers whose prerogative it is to give authoritative informed advice in all areas, from science to accounting to human rights. This group forms a substantial component of the educated elite of any country, but only a small proportion of the overall population. It is supplemented by those who specifically benefit from the protections afforded by liberal policies. Many liberties are worth protecting, but people are not equal in the need to have their liberties protected. Those most in need of protection from the government, and in a democracy from the majority, are the vulnerable members of socially excluded minority groups. Members of these groups disproportionately tend to support liberal parties and policies, if not out of a natural instinct then at least out of a confluence of interests. They share that common interest with the third component of the liberal coalition: the truly wealthy.

The owners of great wealth and property are

predisposed toward liberalism because of the protections its principles afford against expropriation by the masses. Since the time of the ancient Greeks, the wealthy have sought protection against democratic ("mob") rule. Liberalism, with its emphasis on the inviolability of the individual, is one of the forms of protection that is not inherently at odds with democracy itself. The guarantee of due process, the prohibition of bills of attainder (laws directed against specific people), and even freedom of the press are all policies that, while good in their own right, are especially useful for the very wealthy for the protection of their wealth. In the United States the alliance between liberals and the wealthy dates from the birth of the republic. In his 1913 book *The Economic Interpretation of the Constitution of the United States*, the historian Charles Beard calculated that George Washington was probably the richest person in America at the time of his Presidency and one of the largest holders of Revolutionary War bonds, some of which were trading at discounts of 95 percent. No wonder he was a liberal who supported Hamilton's plan to redeem all government debt at face value!

Professionals, minorities, and the wealthy may make for unlikely bedfellows, but together they form the base electoral constituency for liberalism in democratic polities. Broadly speaking, professionals provide the ideas, the wealthy provide the money, and minorities provide the votes. But not all minorities are predisposed to support the liberal agenda. Only the members of socially excluded minorities stand in real need of liberal protections. In the United States, this has always meant African-Americans and Native Americans, but also at various times Irish-Americans, Mormon Americans, Catholic Americans, Jewish Americans, Italian-Americans, Mexican-Americans, Asian Americans, and many others. It has also included non-ethnic, non-religious minorities like homosexuals and the disabled. But with the exception of African-Americans and Native Americans, the roster of socially excluded minorities has been a rotating constituency for liberals as different groups come to be and cease to be socially excluded.

For example, Irish-Americans have long ceased to feel any need for protection against arbitrary majority rule, and consequently have long since dropped out of the liberal coalition. Other minority groups have followed them down the road to social acceptance and social inclusion. When pundits claim that the United States is fast becoming a majority-minority country, they base their logic on the false assumption that the groups identified as socially excluded minorities in the late twentieth century will continue to suffer social exclusion in the twenty-first. That assumption is patently false. Sadly, American society has always been highly racialized to the detriment of African-Americans and Native Americans. That racialization is likely to continue. But other minorities have rotated and will rotate out of the liberal constituency. Minorities don't necessarily vote for liberal candidates. Socially excluded minorities do.

Thus there are never likely to be enough minority voters to make pure liberalism a winning electoral proposition. The authority of experts and the money of the rich ensure that liberal points of view are always prominently aired in political debates, but liberals as a group are never numerically strong enough to win elections held under universal suffrage. In the United States, the liberal Federalist Party narrowly won the first contested Presidential election in 1796, partly on the prestige of George Washington's implicit blessing but also partly due to the system of indirect voting adopted by most Northern states. As American states moved decisively toward apportioning their Presidential electors by universal (white) male suffrage, the Federalist Party collapsed. A similar process occurred in the United Kingdom. The last time the British Liberal Party won a general election was 1910. It was wiped out with the advent of universal male suffrage in 1918.

When electorates are not limited by property qualifications or indirect voting, liberals can only win elections in coalition with other political blocs. When the United Kingdom introduced universal male suffrage, many of its liberals joined the Labour Party. The most famous exception was Winston Churchill. In 1908 the Liberal Party cabinet minister Winston Churchill introduced Britain's first minimum wage legislation and in 1911 he designed its first unemployment insurance program. Only after the Liberal Party collapsed did Churchill became the conservative icon he is today. In the United States liberalism was associated first with the Federalists, then in quick succession with the Whigs and the new Republican Party. For nineteenth-century American Democrats, "liberal" was a dirty word. For example, the profoundly illiberal New York Democratic Party political machine known as Tammany Hall was founded by Alexander Hamilton's arch-enemy Aaron Burr. It dominated the city's politics until 1937, when it was finally put out of business by the (minority) Italian-American liberal Republican Fiorello La Guardia.

The British Conservative Party and the American

Republican Party have had on-again, off-again flirtations with liberalism, but they have always been conservative parties at heart. Similarly, the British Labour Party and the American Democratic Party may have embraced liberalism toward the end of the twentieth century, but historically both were progressive in orientation. In mass democracies with universal suffrage, most of the electorate divides into two groups: the haves (landowners, investors, small business owners) and the have-nots (laborers, students, the unemployed). This is not a straightforward matter of rich versus poor, though the poor are certainly among the have-nots. It is a matter of those who have a substantial stake in the maintenance of the existing system (natural conservatives) versus those who stand to benefit from the revision of the existing system (natural progressives). For the majority of society, liberalism is a side-show. Elections are decided on a conservative–progressive axis.

When liberals strive to protect existing freedoms, they naturally fall in with conservatives. When they seek to establish new rights, they get along much better with progressives. The growth of classical (freedom-focused) liberalism into modern (rights-based) liberalism in the early twentieth century shifted the liberal center of gravity from the conservative to the progressive camp. Accordingly, though nineteenth-century liberals (like Abraham Lincoln and the young Winston Churchill) may have felt more at home with conservative parties, late twentieth-century liberals (like Bill Clinton and Tony Blair) felt more at home with progressive parties. Both British Labour and the American Democrats were progressive before they were liberal, and their voters remain progressive. Witness the popularity of Jeremy Corbyn and Bernie Sanders among the rank and file of their parties, despite the contempt they receive from their respective party elites.

Bill Clinton's New Democrats and Tony Blair's New Labour represented the liberal takeover of the historically progressive parties of the United States and the United Kingdom. Not coincidentally, both takeovers constituted (and were characterized at the time as) the professionalization of the parties. In both parties the professional staff took over from the old believers, and in both parties non-minority progressives – who form the majority of their potential voters – were marginalized. As a result, both party establishments became fully committed to thoroughly liberal, rights-based political agendas (though this is now complicated in the UK by the fact that the Labour Party leader, Jeremy Corbyn, is himself an anti-establishment insurgent). President

Barack Obama's signature domestic policy achievement was a new liberal right to buy healthcare, not a progressive guarantee of free healthcare. Candidate Hillary Clinton's signature domestic policy promise was a liberal offer of citizenship rights to people who had entered the country illegally. Barack Obama and Hillary Clinton are both Democrats, but they are not progressives. They are liberals through and through.

The refugee connection

As a political block that depends on socially excluded minorities for its electoral strength, the liberal coalition is naturally predisposed to favor high levels of immigration. Britain's nineteenth-century Liberal Party aggressively pursued poor Irish voters despite the extreme culture clash between immigrant Irish Catholics and the nonconformist Protestants who made up the bulk of the Liberal Party membership. Open borders are broadly consistent with liberal ideals and liberals' support for immigration certainly goes beyond mere instrumental considerations. Nonetheless it is noteworthy that in non-democratic countries like China, where liberals need not be concerned with assembling a popular coalition, liberals are much less concerned about opening borders and expanding immigrants' rights. Liberal support for immigration seems to be strongest where it is likely to do liberals the most good. For example, there has been remarkably little liberal support in Western democracies for Chinese immigration, despite massive Chinese demand to immigrate. In most Western countries, mainland Chinese immigrants tend to vote conservative.

Among immigrant groups, liberal support is especially strong when it comes to refugees. Again, this is consistent with liberal ideals. It is also an area in which expert authority holds its greatest sway. Experts have little direct input into decisions about immigration for lifestyle, employment, or family reasons. Experts may be consulted in the formulation of policy and may hold nominal responsibility for the approval of individual cases, but the relevant administrative procedures are straightforward and most immigration determinations are made by clerks, not professionals. The situation for refugees is very different. Expert lawyers and judges routinely claim a special authority over refugee policy on the basis of their unique ability to interpret international law. Of course, contemporary international law is in one sense no law at all, since there is no international sovereign to legislate it.

But there is such a thing as international authority. When national courts take cognizance of developing global liberal norms, they in essence defer to the authority of the transnational expert class. And that authority is nowhere proclaimed more loudly than with regard to refugees.

It may seem obvious that refugee status must be determined by experts, but in common English parlance all people seeking refuge are refugees, whether or not they are ultimately successful in obtaining legal recognition of their right to resettlement in the country of their choice. Thus in any common-sense understanding of the word, most refugees never even get the opportunity to plead their cases before judges because most refugees never make it anywhere near their desired countries of refuge. German judges are currently considering the claims of a million or more refugees only because the German Chancellor Angela Merkel made a political decision to invite them in. Had Merkel taken a less liberal political stance, most of those people would not now be in Germany to have their legal cases heard.

For Western countries, particularly the English-speaking ones, the supply of people seeking refuge will always vastly outnumber the willingness of national electorates to admit them. This is strikingly so in Australia, where popular anti-refugee senti-ment is so strong that both major political parties share an unequivocal "stop the boats" policy pledge to block refugee arrivals. In the United States, the otherwise liberal Obama administration threw tens of thousands of refugee children into administra-tive detention in a successful effort to staunch the flow of what they called "unaccompanied children from Central America." The Trump administration is even less welcoming. Across the Atlantic, for more than a decade the United Kingdom steadfastly refused to admit refugees from the "Jungle" in Calais on the French side of the Channel Tunnel. The French authorities finally cleared out the camp in October 2016. These were all political decisions, and right or wrong they were all broadly popular.

Liberal human rights activists and lawyers seek to change this practice. Throughout the 2015 European refugee crisis, as more than a million people responded to Angela Merkel's invitation to settle in Germany, liberals condemned the leaders of Eastern European countries for attempting to maintain control over their borders. Hungary's Prime Minister Viktor Orban was particularly singled out for liberal scorn. Yet in construct-ing a border fence, Orban was doing no more than asserting the sovereignty of the Hungarian state over the sovereignty of European experts. The expert class as one demanded that Hungary permit an unlimited number of refugees to transit Hungarian territory on their way to Germany. None of the refugees wanted to stay in Hungary. Orban could have simply bussed them through, as his Serbian and Macedonian colleagues did. By instead asserting Hungarian sovereignty and the integrity of Hungary's borders, Orban earned the opprobrium of liberals worldwide. But he gained massive domestic democratic legitimacy.

Refugees are among the most vulnerable people in the world and are more in need of liberal protections than almost anyone else. But the current system of state sovereignty excludes the vast majority of the world's refugees and would-be refugees from the protection of the kinds of liberal human rights that can only be guaranteed by state power. A much more robust international legal system would be necessary to protect refugees extraterritorially, giving them not only the right to stay once they enter a country but the right to enter a country in the first place. And such a system, like all claims in international law, can only be made with reference to the authority of experts. The seeds of a transnational sovereignty based on expert authority have already been sown in the practical necessity for family reunion among the refugees who made it to Germany before the borders were closed. Someone will have to decide whether or not the families of more than 100,000 unaccompanied teenage boys will be allowed to join their children in Europe. Those decisions are likely to be made by judges, not by politicians. And they will set new precedents for the transnational reach of the expert class.

3

Liberal Authoritarianism in a Global World

Hungary's Viktor Orban is not the only one building fences. After vigorously condemning Hungary's
fence-building in 2015, most other European countries with borders to the south and east have
now built fences as well, including Austria, whose
Chancellor had (inevitably) previously compared
Hungary's fence to Nazi atrocities. In March 2016
the European Union signed a deal to pay Turkey to
prevent refugees from leaving the country in the first
place, and similar deals have been negotiated with
North African countries. But the biggest border wall
of all has yet to be built: Donald Trump's promised
800-mile wall to fill in the gaps between existing
barriers on the US–Mexico border. If Trump's pro-
posed border wall across the remote deserts of the
American southwest has been perceived as a much
greater threat to international unity than any of

the existing barriers dividing the rich farmlands of Central Europe, it has more to do with the rhetoric than with the reality of the project. Trump's promise to make Mexico pay for the wall may be prima facie ridiculous, but the promise itself is provocative enough to cause alarm.

No one would expect liberals inside or outside the United States to be pleased by the nationalist crowing of the new President of the United States. Indeed, Trump has given them many good reasons to be alarmed. He has wiped clear a decade of work building the Trans-Pacific Partnership (TPP), bullied NATO members into spending more on their own defense, reopened the delicately balanced North American Free Trade Agreement (NAFTA), and withdrawn from the Paris climate change agreement. He has disavowed the very principle of multilateral decision-making. In response, liberals routinely express fears for the future of what they anachronistically call the postwar liberal order. "Anachronistically," because the postwar American world order was anything but liberal. The third quarter of the twentieth century was one of the most illiberal periods in American foreign policy history. Liberalism may have triumphed at home in the civil rights era, but the political space for that triumph was generated by a tightly controlled foreign policy.

America's postwar Presidents offered a consistent choice to the other leaders of the "free" world: America's way or no way at all.

The Marshall Plan to rebuild Europe may have been very generous, but it was not very liberal. It was sold to the Republican Congress as a defense measure. Similarly far removed from being a force for liberal internationalism, NATO was organized to rearm West Germany as an American client state; the membership of authoritarian governments in Greece and Turkey was welcomed so long as they remained staunchly anti-communist. When they didn't, the United States and its allies supported military coups. The United States supported authoritarian regimes in Taiwan, South Korea, and South Vietnam, while working to overthrow leftist governments in Chile, Cuba, Iran, and some would even say Australia. Apartheid South Africa was a close American ally. Japan was occupied, with Okinawa held as ransom to ensure good behavior.

In the decades immediately following World War II, immigration to the United States was severely limited, capped at some of the lowest levels in American history. The foreign-born population of the United States reached an all-time low of less than 5 percent in 1970 (it has since rebounded to 14 percent, just one point below the all-time high of 15 percent recorded in 1890). From 1945 until 1972, the major currencies of the "free world" were tightly controlled in a fixed exchange rate system based on a crawling peg to the US dollar, when they were convertible at all. International trade and investment flows expressed as a proportion of global GDP were lower than at any time before the Great Depression. Most Western economies were dominated by state-owned firms, and most Eastern economies were outright communist. North America, Western Europe, and Japan were widely expected to move toward greater "trilateral" coordination of the global economy, a shift supported by leading American philanthropists and foundations. Academics were actively debating the "convergence thesis" that communist and capitalist societies were evolving toward similar institutions for controlling economic life.

American foreign policy also showed few signs of moving toward the creation of a more "liberal" world order. In the 1950s, Henry Kissinger and the Council on Foreign Relations were advocating the advisability of limited nuclear war, while in the 1960s the Johnson administration bombed Southeast Asia into oblivion in an effort to stabilize the political situation in Vietnam. No one would accuse Richard Nixon of being a liberal or an internationalist. The birth of the liberal internationalist world order had to wait until the Presidency of Jimmy Carter and his appointment of Zbigniew Brzezinski as his National Security Advisor. Only in the second half of the 1970s did support for multilateral institutions and democratic freedoms become an important element of American foreign policy, and it took at least two decades of uphill struggle for them to become dominant.

You couldn't ask for a President more different in style from Jimmy Carter than Ronald Reagan, but Reagan essentially continued the Carter/Brzezinski program of a foreign policy based on muscular support for freedom, particularly in Eastern Europe. Reagan also reinforced the authority of the International Monetary Fund, which had been severely undermined in the 1970s by Nixon's suspension of the dollar's convertibility into gold and Carter's inflationary domestic policies. Under George H.W. Bush, the Reagan freedom agenda imperceptibly morphed into the Clinton rights agenda after the fall of the Soviet Union. It was only in the 1990s – not in the postwar era – that the Clinton administration gave birth to the liberal international order as we know it today, an order that continued to expand even under the conspicuously illiberal Presidency of George W. Bush.

The multilateral liberal international system has now enjoyed a quarter-century heyday of its own (the Presidency of George W. Bush notwithstanding), and a generation of liberal internationalist scholars, lawyers, pundits, and activists have come to view it as the natural order of things. Trump threatens all that. And thus with no apparent sense of irony, many liberals have turned to China for support. A flurry of commentary in the world's policy journals glowingly contrasted Chinese President Xi Jinping's internationalist January 17, 2017, speech to the World Economic Forum with Trump's nativist inaugural address three days later. The world's great and good, assembled in the exclusive ski resort of Davos, Switzerland, heard Xi mangle *A Tale of Two Cities* (the book is about the French Revolution, not the Industrial Revolution) and bemoan the world's "widening income gap" (Xi's family wealth was estimated at over $1 billion when he became the world's senior communist five years ago).

At Davos, Xi proclaimed that the world "should develop a model of fair and equitable governance in keeping with the trend of the times" because "[w]hether you like it or not ... [a]ny attempt to cut off the flow of capital, technologies, products, industries and people between economies ... is simply not possible." While implicitly criticizing Trump for his promise (since fulfilled) to withdraw from the Paris climate agreement, Xi endorsed a rules-based international order: "We should adhere to multilateralism to uphold the authority and efficacy of multilateral institutions. We should honor promises and abide by rules." He did not mention China's disavowal of a Permanent Court of Arbitration ruling against its creation of artificial islands in the South China Sea, nor did he mention the lack of "fair and equitable governance" in China itself. No matter. When Xi claims that he is "committed to developing global free trade and investment" and will "say no to protectionism" there is no reason to doubt him. China fully embraces the liberal rights to truck, barter, and exchange. China's people don't lack liberal rights like paid maternity leave. What they lack are basic freedoms – and, of course, democracy.

Democracy versus free trade

Economic rights are the bread and butter of the liberal internationalist agenda, and the most cherished and sacrosanct of these rights has come to be free trade. Free trade is the one issue that more than any other drives a wedge between liberals and progressives. Rightly or wrongly, progressives usually see free trade as an attack on workers' livelihoods, while liberals see it as a matter of sheer common sense. In the 2016 US Presidential election, the progressive insurgent Bernie Sanders' relentless opposition to the TPP negotiated by the Obama administration ultimately forced candidate Clinton to back away from a deal she had previously called "gold standard" (as it happens, another one-time liberal policy priority). It's not only progressives who have historically opposed free trade. Conservatives, too, have often opposed trade deals as undermining economic sovereignty and traditional power structures. It is worth remembering that the Republican Party was the party of high tariffs from its founding in the 1850s until liberals succeeded in making opposition to free trade intellectually disreputable in the 1990s.

But the classic battle between liberals and conservatives over free trade was fought in the United Kingdom. In the nineteenth century, one of the defining issues of the early Conservative Party was its support for restrictions on imported grain. These Corn Laws helped maintain the traditional social, economic, and political structure of the English countryside. They were a primary target for the early Liberal Party.

Free trade in the context of the Corn Laws was at the core of the classic liberal agenda because it was construed as a freedom: the freedom to buy the lowest-priced grain no matter where it came from. It was not a right like the European Union's right to sell products in all member states. Nineteenth-century British liberals did not advocate that Russians and Americans be given the right to sell grain in the United Kingdom. They merely advocated that British citizens have the freedom to buy grain from anyone they chose. American revolutionaries in liberal New England once demanded the same freedom with respect to tea. What freedom of speech is for the professional wing of the expert class, free trade is for the managerial. The human rights activists and CEOs who attend the World Economic Forum meetings at Davos get along just fine when it comes to free trade. In fact, the most powerful liberal argument in Britain's Corn Law debate was that high grain prices disproportionately harmed the poor.

As liberalism has evolved over the last two centuries, so have trade deals. Once concerned with the expansion of freedoms, they are now focused on the determination of rights. For example, the dear departed TPP would have governed the right to the exclusive use of intellectual property (including patents, trademarks, and copyrights), the right to invest in companies and operate businesses in foreign jurisdictions, and the right to trial by international expert panel rather than in each country's court system. As a result the TPP was no more a trade deal than the EU is a customs union. At least the EU includes some popularly elected institutions. The TPP, of course, had none. The TPP would have replaced the direct democratic accountability of national governments with the unaccountable transnational sovereignty of experts. That outcome is not at all illiberal. It is reasonable to argue that the safeguards for economic rights written into the TPP represented a step forward for individual liberty. But the transfer of economic governance functions from democratically elected governments to transnational expert panels would clearly have been a step backward for democracy.

Of course, Trump vetoed the TPP. Many liberals – including Hillary Clinton – have now also distanced themselves from trade agreements. But the disavowal of a liberal goal out of fear of a populist backlash does nothing to change the class interest that underlies the goal of free trade. Deep trade agreements like the TPP that go far beyond the simple elimination of tariffs are consistent with the larger liberal ideal of government by experts. This is not to say that government by experts produces bad outcomes. The perhaps uncomfortable truth is that expert arbitrators operating in secret away from public scrutiny and the rough and tumble of democratic politics may be better able than democratically accountable politicians to resolve trade disputes in a fair and efficient manner. It may also be true that governments are right to negotiate trade agreements in secret, because populist politics would otherwise make it impossible for democratic governments to reach agreement. The technical efficiency of the liberal agenda is not beyond question, but nor is it the focus of populist critique. The key populist objection to the liberal trade agenda is its authoritarianism.

Free trade was a progressive issue when the British Liberal Party took it up in the fight against the Corn Laws. At times it has also become a conservative issue, as when the NAFTA was ratified with disproportionately Republican support in part because it promised to undermine the power of labor unions. But free trade has always been a liberal issue. The increasing interconnectedness of the global economy over the last fifty years has empowered liberals by moving a substantial proportion of economic life out of the national realm (where it is subject to political oversight and interference) and into the transnational ether (where it is governed on the authority of experts). This reinforces both the position of liberals within political parties and the prestige of the expert class itself. The victories of New Labour and the New Democrats in the 1990s were only made possible by the money and skills brought into these parties by their liberal wings. The money at least was tied to the acceptance of free trade. A quarter century later, these erstwhile progressive parties are paying a steep electoral price. Having accepted a liberal agenda in exchange for temporary electoral advantages, Labour and the Democrats now find themselves out of office while at the same time out of ideas.

The globalization of expertise

The liberal internationalist embrace of Xi Jinping as a free trader is emblematic of contemporary liberalism's prioritization of economic rights over basic freedoms. China does in fact grant its people an expanding roster of rights, from the right to basic healthcare to the right to hold foreign currency to the increasing right of Chinese people to choose where to live. In 2016 China even granted its people the right to have two children, instead of just one.

In China rights are granted to people on a techno-cratic basis, when experts judge them appropriate. When China's problem was overpopulation, the right to procreate was limited. Now that the threat has shifted toward underpopulation, the right to procreate is being expanded. Rule by experts makes China a comfortable place for the liberal members of the global expert class. They can offer advice to the Chinese government in the reasonable expecta-tion that the government will listen. China may be an increasingly militarist police state founded on the authority of a ubiquitous communist party, but at least its leaders are not know-nothing nativists like Trump. They are well-traveled, polite, sophis-ticated, highly educated technocrats. They are, if nothing else, experts.

China's expert class was harshly treated during Mao Zedong's Cultural Revolution. Like many other professionals and children of professionals, the teenage Xi Jinping was pulled out of high school and sent to the countryside to learn farm labor. How times have changed. Today experts are once again respected in China, and the upper echelons of China's expert class are coming to be integrated with the global expert class. They attend Ivy League universities, hold top positions in international organizations, and participate in the

World Economic Forum. They've even established their own Davos clone, the Boao Forum for Asia. Reestablished as authorities in their own country, they are coming to be accepted as authorities in the world at large. They are also coming to control great wealth. If there is a global liberal coalition that links experts, plutocrats, and socially excluded minorities, it includes China's top government officials on two out of three counts.

It's no surprise that rich, educated Chinese are welcome in liberal internationalist circles. Liberalism is inherently internationalist because the world's liberals often have more in common with each other than they do with their respective compatriots. This is true for all three components of the liberal coalition. The very rich are a global class, obviously. Socially excluded minorities are often socially excluded precisely because they are of foreign origin or because they have transnational identities. Non-immigrant minorities may also share experiences across borders; for example, gay rights activists in all countries march under the same rainbow flag. But the expert class is coming to be the most globalized group of all. As transnational corporations and other leading organizations come to operate on a global basis, the status hierarchies in which top experts compete for prestige and influence are no longer national, but global.

This is nowhere more true than in education. Global professionals are increasingly educated in English at the world's top-ranked universities, not in their own countries or their own languages. The best schools to have on your professional CV are concentrated in the Anglo-American core of the liberal international system. Most of them are located in the liberal bastions of the northeastern United States and California, with outposts in Oxford, Cambridge, and London, the most liberal cities in England. According to China's semi-official ranking system, the Academic Ranking of World Universities, 23 of the top 25 universities in the world are in English-speaking countries, 19 of them in the United States, 3 in England, and 1 in Canada (the other 2 are in Switzerland and Japan). In a major shift from the pre-globalization world of the twentieth century, these universities now educate the bulk of the world's elite professionals, regardless of nationality. Xi Jinping was educated at China's elite Tsinghua University. His daughter went to Harvard.

The cosmopolitanism of today's global expert class is what makes populist nativism so abhorrent to them. Their political liberalism goes beyond the instinctive affinity for personal freedoms and human rights that comes from years of higher education, reinforced by the natural propensity of experts to embrace a political ideology that looks to them as the authoritative sources of wisdom. The link between liberalism and the globalization of expertise operates at the more visceral level of self-preservation. The world's leading experts in every field are the greatest beneficiaries of transnational liberal rights like the right to invest across borders, the right to intellectual property protection, the right to have disputes resolved outside of potentially biased national court systems, the right of non-discrimination in employment, and the right to work in the country of one's choice. Personal mobility enables professionals to shop for freedoms, and even citizenships, when the governments in their home countries prove unsatisfactory.

The global expert class has every incentive to promote the decision-making authority of its own members and the institutions they control. This innate authoritarianism threatens the effective practice of national sovereignty and has the potential to undermine the popular democracies that depend on it. The main issue is not the formal legal right of countries to make decisions in a democratic manner, though in some countries that may be threatened, particularly in the smaller countries of the European Union. Much more serious is the restriction in the universe of policy options made available by the expert class. Even a free and democratic country needs someone to offer choices to the voters. When every candidate offers basically the same set of policies, differing only in color and flavor but not in substance, democracy is compromised. When the people make democratic choices that their elites refuse to implement, democracy is dead.

All roads lead from Rome

The 1957 Treaty of Rome that established the European Economic Community (precursor to today's European Union) was negotiated in closed session at a chateau outside Brussels. In an inadvertently symbolic statement, the preamble to the treaty states that the King of Belgium, the Presidents of Germany, France, and Italy, the Grand Duchess of Luxembourg, and the Queen of the Netherlands "HAVE DECIDED to create a European Economic Community." The "peoples of Europe" are only mentioned as subjects of the treaty, not authors. The first sentence of the first article of the treaty states that "the High Contracting Parties [i.e., the heads of state] establish among themselves" the European Union. From one point of view this is all just irrelevant rhetoric; from a legal standpoint it doesn't really matter in whose name the European Union was formed. From another point of view, it set a tone for the whole European project that persists to this day.

The European Economic Community absorbed the preexisting European Court of Justice (ECJ) as its judicial arm. As in the United States, it was not initially clear that the ECJ would have the power of judicial supremacy. There is no explicit statement in the Treaty of Rome of the supremacy of ECJ rulings over those of national courts. The ECJ arrogated to itself the power of judicial supremacy over the member states' national institutions in 1964, and in practice its authority has never been seriously questioned. Considering that by 1957 judicial supremacy had been a topic of heated legal debate in the United States for more than 150 years, the drafters of the Treaty of Rome might reasonably have been expected to address it, unless perhaps they felt that an explicit statement of European legal supremacy over national institutions might have been politically inexpedient. They did find time to specify that the staff of the ECJ must "be chosen from among persons of indisputable independence" – in other words, they must be apolitical experts, not political appointees. That may be very sensible, but it is not necessarily very democratic.

The European Union has from the beginning been a highly authoritarian institution in the best sense of the term: it is constitutionally predisposed to govern on the basis of expert authority. In that it is no different from many United Nations bodies or indeed the People's Republic of China. In theory the European Union may be beholden to the governments of its member states, but in practice European Union policies are not shaped by democratic debate and are only distantly subject to democratic oversight. Of course countries are represented in European institutions, and through their countries, voters are as well. But that chain of representation is a fudge at best, a fig leaf at worst. Democratic elections in member states are rarely contested on the basis of what position the elected government will take on specific aspects of EU governance. At most, parties may be "pro-EU" or "anti-EU." This contrasts strongly with parties' positions on national policies. All Polish political parties are "pro-Poland" but some are for higher pensions, others for tax cuts. Across the EU, national policies are subject to intense democratic scrutiny. European issues get only a thumbs-up or thumbs-down hearing – and when it's thumbs-down, all Hell breaks loose.

The most egregious example of "all Hell" was the popular rejection in 2005 of the European Union Constitutional Treaty. European Union legal experts spent three years drafting a European Union Constitution to consolidate the patchwork of existing European treaties and institutions into a single, unified body of law. As a new treaty, the Constitution had to be ratified by all 25 then-member states to take effect. Given the sweeping scope of the treaty, several member states opted to ratify it by popular referendum rather than by Parliamentary legislation. They expected an easy ride. The treaty was supported by all of Europe's major political parties, the mainstream press, academics, and the business community. In short, the entire expert class endorsed the new European Constitution. But first in France and then with an even bigger majority in the Netherlands the voters rejected the treaty.

When the European expert class failed to win a democratic mandate, they went back to the drawing boards – not to meet the voters' objections (which they considered irrational) but to find a way to circumvent them. The resulting 2007 Treaty of Lisbon implemented much of the originally intended European Constitution as a series of amendments to existing treaties rather than as a new basic law. Only the Irish government was brave enough to allow a referendum on the treaty, and the Irish people voted it down on June 12, 2008. Soon afterward the global financial crisis struck Ireland, decimating the Irish economy and driving the unemployment rate up from 5 percent to 15 percent. It was in this context that the Irish government held a second referendum on October 2, 2009, with the Irish political establishment warning people that they faced further economic hardship if they persisted in their resistance. The people duly capitulated. Ireland was in, the treaty was saved, and EU institutions were transformed in the direction demanded by Europe's expert class.

This sordid story of progress toward the "ever closer union among the peoples of Europe" does not unequivocally demonstrate that European integration is wrong or even that the people of Europe do not genuinely desire greater integration. What it does demonstrate is that the European expert class routinely and successfully places its authoritative judgments above democratic review by ordinary citizens. Looking across all of Europe, only in the UK has the expert class (tentatively) accepted the democratic repudiation of its authoritative advice, and even there the ultimate implementation of the 2016 Brexit referendum verdict is still in doubt, though it is hard to imagine that the British political class would follow the Irish path of supporting the EU against its own people. Within the UK, the English nation in particular has a long history of successful resistance to authoritarian outsiders, be they Spanish, French, German, or "European." Overt authoritarianism doesn't go down any better in England than it does in the United States.

Back in Davos, Xi Jinping emphasized that when it comes to charting a country's path to social and economic development "All roads lead to Rome." He meant to imply that today's liberal internationalist world could accommodate many different forms of government, including China's totalitarian one-party dictatorship. But the aphorism has an older meaning in its Latin original: the implication that no matter what direction you think you are traveling, you have no choice but to end up in Rome. When liberals place their own policy positions beyond democratic review, they are as surely authoritarian as the dictator who turns to the church or the army for support. In individual national democracies, liberal authoritarianism is often held in check by populism, and though populists rarely win they do make the running. At the global level, liberals face fewer obstacles. Populists are thin on the ground at intergovernmental alphabet agencies like the IMF, the BIS, the ECB, and the OECD, to say nothing of influential non-governmental organizations like the WEF.

The old authoritarianisms have repeatedly threatened and occasionally overthrown democracies in many countries, though noticeably not in the Anglo-Saxon world. Liberal authoritarianism has been more patient but may ultimately prove more successful. The new liberal authoritarianism, acting at the global level, is perhaps the most dangerous authoritarianism of all. Not dangerous for humanity; more often than not, liberal internationalists legislate in the best interests of humanity. No, the new liberal authoritarianism is dangerous for democracy. Whether we prefer to live in good dictatorships or questionable democracies is (perhaps) for us to decide. But global governance is no democracy. It is the private preserve of the global expert class.

4

The Passion of Donald J. Trump

If there's one thing that liberal internationalists found most revolting in Donald Trump's inaugural address, it was Trump's pledge that "From this moment on, it's going to be America First." For them, "America First" was an abomination. But long before the twenty-first-century Republican Party turned nativist, it was the progressive wing of the Democratic Party that embraced economic nationalism. Toward the end of the nineteenth century, liberal internationalists sought to create what was, in essence, the world's first global currency by convincing all of the countries of the world to adopt the gold standard. Imagine a global Euro. In the US election of 1896, the gold standard debate split the Democratic Party into a globalist "sound money" gold standard faction and a nationalist "inflationary" silver standard faction. The candidate of the nationalists, William Jennings Bryan, decried the influence of global bankers, declaring that "this nation is able to legislate for its own people on every question without waiting for the aid or consent of any other nation on earth."

The arch-populist Bryan won the Democratic nomination by a landslide, though he went on to lose the general election to the gold standard Republican William McKinley. Bryan's 1896 "Cross of Gold" speech, however, became one of the most famous in American political history. Blaming the gold standard for bankrupting farmers and causing the depression, Bryan concluded his speech with the immortal indictment "You shall not press down upon the brow of labor this crown of thorns; you shall not crucify mankind upon a cross of gold." And though Bryan lost the election, history would ultimately prove him right. With the outbreak of World War I in 1914, the gold standard proved unsustainable. The return to the gold standard in the 1920s is widely believed to have been a major cause of the Great Depression.

Tellingly, the final act of Bryan's life in public service was to act as counsel for the prosecution in the famous 1925 Scopes "Monkey Trial," in which Bryan helped prosecute high-school teacher John T. Scopes for breaking a Tennessee law against the teaching of evolution in public schools. Scopes was defended by the American Civil Liberties Union. As the Scopes trial illustrates, old-time Democrats were more likely to be Christian fundamentalists than liberal human rights advocates. Like FDR in a later generation, Bryan was a progressive but he was no liberal. He was an unabashed populist.

Liberal pundits like to link populism with authoritarianism, but in fact they are polar opposite strategies for political legitimation. Populists appeal to the innate common sense of ordinary people, while authoritarians appeal to tradition and the prestige of established institutions. Thus while populism is a natural strategy for progressives, authoritarianism tends to work well for conservatives. Of course, just as most progressives are not populists, most conservatives are not authoritarians. What populism and authoritarianism have in common is that both are "know-nothing" strategies that disdain sophisticated arguments and appeal instead to voters' more visceral instincts. Populism appeals to the voters' immediate needs (often the need to make a living) while authoritarianism appeals to their larger loyalties (particularly to their religious faith). Neither appeals to logic, which is why liberals despise them so much – and perhaps why liberals so often incorrectly lump them together. Few politicians have ever managed to pull off a populist authoritarianism. Adolf Hitler may have been the only one. And when you want to vilify your opponents, you can't ask for a better straw man than Adolf Hitler.

Whereas Bryan was a natural progressive populist, Donald Trump belongs to that rarer breed: the conservative populist. Bryan and Trump may belong to opposing political traditions, but they share a common political style. Like Trump, Bryan was pilloried in the liberal press as a narcissist hungry for power and concerned only with his own self-promotion. Like Trump, Bryan disingenuously promised to put millions of unemployed back to work. Like Trump, Bryan's program was big on rhetoric but sketchy on details. But the progressive Bryan is remembered as a hero of the American working class because he promised to bring down the plutocracy of the rich. Trump will never be a hero to anyone but himself. As a billionaire property developer and television personality who has appointed a slew of financiers to his cabinet, Trump can hardly claim to be a man of the people. The Trump agenda will preserve wealth, perhaps even create wealth, but it will definitely not redistribute wealth.

Trump may be a conservative, but as a populist

he is a very different kind of conservative from those who embrace authoritarianism. Anyone calling Trump an authoritarian has one simple question to answer: to what authority does Donald Trump defer? Spain's Francisco Franco and Portugal's Antonio Salazar turned to the church and the army for support, as did France's more mildly authoritarian Charles de Gaulle. Hitler and Stalin had their totalitarian political parties. Xi Jinping is overseeing a delicate transition from a communist authoritarianism to a new kind of Confucian authoritarianism. Russia's Vladimir Putin founded his regime on the authority of the security services buttressed by a revival of orthodox religion, and Turkey's Recep Tayyip Erdogan founded his regime on the authority of orthodox religion buttressed by the security services. Poland's much milder authoritarian, Jaroslaw Kaczynski, trades on the moral authority of the Catholic church and the Solidarity trade union movement.

Donald J. Trump defers to no authority other than Donald J. Trump. His speeches and interviews are suffused with paeans to his own greatness. He did not demand that voters support him because of their deep-seated commitment to traditional institutions. Nearly all of those institutions were arrayed against him. Trump did not portray himself as the preserver of the faith, whether that faith be religious or party-based. He asked that people put their faith in him, personally. Donald Trump is a populist (and a narcissist), but you can't be an authoritarian when the only authority you recognize is yourself.

The routine liberal equation of Donald Trump with Adolf Hitler is as false as it is outrageous. Trump is not the charismatic leader of a totalitarian political party. He does not command a paramilitary cadre of uniformed thugs. Embarrassingly for Trump's liberal critics, the only election-related gang violence in 2016 seems to have been the abduction and torture in Chicago of a disabled white teenager by four black classmates. There are no signs that Trump is anti-Semitic. The reality is that Trump is aggressively pro-Israel and was warmly welcomed in Jerusalem by Israeli Prime Minister Benjamin Netanyahu. In fact, the rabbi who gave the blessing at Trump's inauguration was himself the target of hundreds of online anti-Semitic slurs. It is true that the Ku Klux Klan, many overt racists, and several neo-Nazi groups came out in support of Trump's campaign, but such groups have routinely endorsed Republican candidates since the beginning of the civil rights era. Trump has disavowed their support just as other Republican candidates have, even if he was unacceptably slow to do so.

Charges of Nazism are thrown around far too casually in politics, as Hitler and the Nazis have degenerated into a kind of comic-book shorthand for the historical realization of absolute evil. The idea that Donald Trump is a latter-day Lucifer disguised as a reality TV star is as laughable as (in many ways) is Donald Trump himself. Comparison with Hitler is a cheap way to insult a politician, and the qualification of degree ("reminiscent of Hitler") is a cowardly way to shield the insulter from accusations of libel while still pushing home the point. Will Trump really build a wall on the Mexican border? Perhaps. Will he invade Mexico, exterminate its people, and settle white supremacists on their expropriated land? That is the implication of comparing Trump with Hitler. Hitler would do just that.

From popular sovereignty to exclusionary nativism

Trump's supposed genocidal racism is associated by liberals with his call for suspending the issuance of visas to citizens of a rotating roster of Muslim-majority countries and his plans to build a wall along the Mexican border – i.e., with his support for greater immigration controls. Trump does in fact disagree with the liberal agenda for increased immigration and the admission to citizenship of illegal immigrants already residing in the United States. Even if there were not sound empirical rationales for these policies they would not be inherently racist, but nativist. Nativism ("America first") is an illiberal political philosophy that espouses the prioritization of the needs and preferences of the existing citizens of a country over the needs and preferences of prospective future citizens and of the outside world in general. Nativism may be illiberal, but in its benign aspect as the prioritization of the wants and needs of the members of a particular political community over those of non-members it is the very foundation of popular sovereignty.

Where the people are sovereign – as they notionally are in the United States – nativism is constitutionally enshrined in the political system. The first three words of the United States Constitution, "We the People," implicitly exclude all who are not among "the People." The Article II restriction of the Presidency to "natural born" citizens (people who have been citizens from birth) further emphasizes the inherent nativism of the American political system. The French system of state sovereignty and the British system of Parliamentary sovereignty are more equivocal on this. For example, in the colonial era it was long unclear to what extent the non-white populations of India and Jamaica were "British," an ambiguity made possible by the early location of sovereignty in Parliament rather than in a specific population. Similarly, when France and other continental European countries conquered foreign territories, the rights of the conquered people were not always well defined. In any state that has "subjects" rather than "citizens," the debate over special rights for natives is muted, since it is no great honor to be the subject of such a state.

Nativism has always been a prominent element of American political culture because in the United States the people have always been sovereign, reserving substantial freedoms for themselves and granting (limited) rights to the governments that govern them. The liberal equation of nativism with racism is consistent with the liberal preference for expert sovereignty over popular sovereignty. Popular sovereignty is by definition exclusionary, but it only becomes genocidal when one political community decides to murder other political communities that share the same territory, as in the Rwandan genocide of 1994 and the attempted Bosnian genocide of 1992–1996. The United States has its own dark history of the genocide of Native

Americans, which long predated the Nazi genocide of European Jewry. Given this sorry record, liberals may be correct to associate popular sovereignty with a historical propensity to genocide. That said, no one seriously expects Donald Trump's America to turn genocidal on the model of Nazi Germany, or even of the American frontier.

Racism, however, is another matter. Nativism may be only potentially genocidal, but it is inherently exclusionary, and in effect racist in those nations that construct their identities in racial terms. In multi-racial America, nativism is not inherently racist, and can be distinguished from racism. African-Americans face severe racial discrimination, but this is not tied to an assertion of their non-membership in the body politic. The days of "back to Africa" are long gone. Thus while liberals may be right to associate nativism with racism in many countries, they are wrong to do so in the United States. Trump's immigration proposals are nativist, but they are not inherently racist. They might even be called technocratic. The overwhelming majority of foreign terrorist attacks on US citizens do seem to originate in Muslim-majority countries. And the only country from which a large number of people illegally enter the United States via a land border is Mexico. It seems obvious that any sensible approach to border control in the United States should pay special attention to Muslim-majority countries and border crossings from Mexico. Racism is a red herring.

In Britain, too, nativism has been incorrectly branded as racism. In the debate over the 2016 Brexit referendum, anti-immigration "Leave" advocates have routinely been characterized as racist by expert commentators on the "Remain" side, flagrantly ignoring the obvious fact that most European Union immigrants to the United Kingdom are white. Many of the lowest-paid British workers at risk of displacement by those white newcomers are themselves of South Asian origin – i.e., non-white. In this context, nativism clearly cannot be equated with racism.

The Brexit referendum was in effect a contest between the popular nativism of the Leavers and the liberal inclusion of the Remainers. David Cameron's use of the referendum as a political tool was in effect if not in law a partial transfer of sovereignty from Parliament to the people. He made that transfer because he was incorrectly confident of a result that would confirm his liberal internationalist position without his having to be the one to assert it. The British people instead embraced a more nativist view of British sovereignty and voted to leave the European Union. The expert class on both sides of the Channel reacted with shock, dismay – and fury. They suggested that the elderly and the less educated were not qualified to vote on such a complicated issue. They attempted to use the courts to delay or obstruct the implementation of the referendum decision, and attempted to persuade Parliament to overrule the people's (non-binding) verdict. If Brexit proceeds, they will almost certainly seek redress from the European Court of Justice on one of a number of technicalities regarding the rights of EU citizens. British, European, and global liberals are unified in their condemnation of Brexit nativism and horrified that their authority has been defied.

Yet even leaving aside people's understandable attachment to national sovereignty, elderly and less-educated Britons may have been entirely rational to vote "Leave." The EU right to work in continental European countries has little value for them. What British grocery store clerk or retiree is ever going to work in Paris or Berlin? But the right of other EU citizens to work in the United Kingdom compromises their income-earning potential, and that of their children and grandchildren. These homespun truths, so clear to ordinary working people, seem invisible to the world's experts. The experts may call British "Leave" voters bigoted, xenophobic, and (of course) racist, but in the end these are just insulting liberal synonyms for "exclusionary." The British people made a socially exclusionary decision when they voted to leave the European Union. In effect they voted to withdraw the unlimited right to work in the UK that their government had granted to the citizens of other EU countries, including ten new, relatively poor EU member states in 2004. Bearing in mind the catastrophic impact of that decision on the job opportunities of ordinary British citizens, it's easy to see why they did.

Populism and the paranoid style

Donald Trump's inauguration speech is unlikely to be remembered as one of America's great political speeches, but it is already being studied as one of its most distinctive. Liberal internationalists have tried to draw parallels between it and Hitler's infamous Nuremberg speech and to link the speech to 1930s American Nazi sympathizers, mainly on the strength of his "America first" slogan. But "America first" has a pedigree that goes all the way back to Washington's farewell address, and in any case most ordinary Americans fail to see any inherent evil in the idea of an American President putting America first. Liberal internationalism has a long and distinguished intellectual pedigree, but Trump's critics are wrong to suggest that only the Nazis have ever opposed it. Compare Trump's "right of all nations to put their own interests first" with William Jennings Bryan's threat that no one "can protect from the avenging wrath of an indignant people the man . . . who is willing to surrender the right of self-government and place legislative control in the hands of foreign potentates and powers." Trump may lack Bryan's soaring rhetoric but his sentiments are the same.

The difference between the "America first" of George Washington and Woodrow Wilson, on the one hand, and William Jennings Bryan and Donald Trump, on the other, is that the Bryan/Trump brand of nativism is overtly populist. Trump assumed the mantle of the people when he claimed in his inaugural address that "we are not merely transferring power from one administration to another, or from one party to another – but we are transferring power from Washington, DC and giving it back to you, the American People." Bryan did not win election to the Presidency but he painted his campaign in similar colors: "Old leaders have been cast aside when they refused to give expression to the sentiments of those whom they would lead, and new leaders have sprung up to give direction to this cause of freedom." Railing against the political influence of big business, Bryan identified himself with the anger of ordinary workers: "We beg no longer; we entreat no more; we petition no more. We defy them!" Trump's conservative policy program is the polar opposite of Bryan's progressive agenda, but the two men share a single style.

The Presidential historian Richard Hofstadter called it the "paranoid style" in a famous 1964 essay in *Harper's* magazine. He was writing about Barry Goldwater, but he emphasized that the paranoid style wasn't limited to conservatives. Hofstadter characterized it as a combination of "heated exaggeration, suspiciousness, and conspiratorial fantasy," often directed against "international bankers" and other easy populist targets. Hofstadter was too respectful (or perhaps strategic) to name William Jennings Bryan, but he did use an 1895 populist manifesto against the gold standard as one of his key examples of the paranoid style. Bryan's own language in the Cross of Gold speech was no less incendiary. What's more, he reportedly ended the speech by holding his arms out to his side and bowing his head as if being crucified himself – and held the pose in silence for a full five seconds as the audience sat spellbound.

Trump may be a latter-day populist, but Bryan was the original article.

Like Bryan and Roosevelt in previous centuries, Trump is a paranoid populist with a persecution complex. Roosevelt was the direct political heir of Bryan, picking up Bryan's program of inflationary spending, a high income tax, and even the removal of elderly justices from the Supreme Court. Like Bryan, Roosevelt was bitterly resented by the country's moneyed elite. In its tone of resistance to Hofstadter's "international bankers" Roosevelt's Second New Deal speech might have been lifted directly from the Cross of Gold: "Never before in all our history have these forces been so united against one candidate as they stand today. They are unanimous in their hate for me – and I welcome their hatred." If Wall Street bankers were unanimous in their hatred for Bryan and Roosevelt, liberal intellectuals are unanimous in their hatred for Donald Trump. That hatred goes well beyond disagreement; liberal intellectuals would have disagreed with the policies of any of the 2016 Republican candidates for President. It is hatred on the level of the liberal reaction against Brexit in the United Kingdom, but directed against a single man rather than a broad class. It is the hatred of people who feel their position in society has been undermined.

The Passion of Donald J. Trump

Whether or not the many misconduct accusations leveled at Donald Trump turn out to be true, Trump is right to feel unfairly persecuted by the press and liberal civil society. His record strongly suggests that he is a misogynist who does not behave appropriately around "beautiful" (his word) women. Certainly a more decorous record would be preferred in the President of the United States. But it seems unlikely that the degree of hatred directed against Trump can be explained by the extent of his alleged misconduct. After all, Bill Clinton's well-established sexual depredation of subordinates would have resulted in his dismissal from any ordinary professional position (lawyer, academic, or journalist). There was no Women's March on Washington to demand his resignation. Quite the contrary: most women's groups supported him against impeachment by an obviously disingenuous Republican Congress. The difference is that whereas Bill Clinton preyed on individual women, Donald Trump challenged the authority of liberal female professionals to speak for American women as a whole.

Given that Hillary Clinton was the first female major party Presidential candidate in American history, one would have expected her to attract a disproportionate number of women voters or at least to energize more women to vote. She did not. Clinton won roughly the same proportion of women voters as Barack Obama and Al Gore and (adding insult to irony) a smaller proportion than Bill Clinton won in 1996. Hillary Clinton won large majorities among African-American and Hispanic-American women, but these majorities were smaller than those won four years earlier by Barack Obama. Clinton scored a modest 6-point victory over Trump among university-educated white women but Trump won an 18-point victory among less-educated white women. A million or more women may have marched against the Trump Presidency on January 21, 2017, but they are extremely unlikely to have been representative of American women as a whole. For the women who marched, that must have been frustrating indeed.

The mystery of Hillary Clinton's failure to attract more female voters can't be attributed simply to her personal unlikability. Clinton may have been the second least popular candidate in American polling history, but Donald Trump was the first. Had Clinton won a landslide among women voters, as experts expected and as she implicitly demanded in her campaign rhetoric, she would have coasted to the Presidency. She dedicated her concession speech to "all the little girls who are watching this," promising that although "we have still not shattered that highest and hardest glass ceiling" someone eventually would. That dedication betrays exactly where she went wrong. Far more women's careers are limited by stagnant wages and pervasive underemployment than by their inability to become President of the United States. Clinton's belief that her victory would have represented an advance for all women was apparently not shared by many American women, and certainly not by the majority of less-educated white women. They placed their faith instead in the alleged rapist Donald Trump.

Sociologists have a term for this: false consciousness. If less-educated women do not share a strong sense of solidarity with other members of their gender, if they do not celebrate the achievements of a fellow woman like Hillary Clinton, they are accused of having a false consciousness of themselves as being something other than first and foremost female. Whatever the moral merits of this kind of argument, it fails as sociology because being female is generally not the most important determinant of a woman's status in society. That's why Hillary Clinton did not mobilize women the way Barack Obama mobilized African-Americans. In 2008 many white Americans had trouble understanding why it was considered acceptable for

African-Americans to support Barack Obama based on his skin color but not acceptable for whites to do the same for John McCain. The difference is that the presence of Barack Obama in the Oval Office broke down many of the racial barriers that separated African-Americans from white Americans. The election of John McCain would have had no such impact. The success of Barack Obama was, and was perceived to be, symbolically important for all African-Americans because African-Americans are a socially excluded minority. Unlike African-Americans, women are not.

Women are a majority, and one that is fully integrated into the vast majority of American families. Women face systematic discrimination, hardship, and violence, but there are no female ghettos, female-dominated school systems, or female-dominated prison systems. Women were once socially excluded, and it was once possible to organize women on a class basis to fight for women's rights. But women's social exclusion was never as severe as that faced by African-Americans, and the extension of full civil rights to women has reduced female social exclusion to the point where most women now have much more in common with the men in their families than they do with elite female politicians like Hillary Clinton. This does not imply that women have achieved real equality with men, or that violence against women has ceased to be a major social problem. It only means that the election of Hillary Clinton would have done little to fix these problems. And so African-Americans, who have much more at stake in the success of the liberal coalition than women do, voted overwhelmingly for Hillary Clinton. American women, who have much less need of liberal protections, did not.

Less-educated American women instead joined their fathers, brothers, husbands, and sons in voting for Donald Trump. They accepted his story of persecution at the hands of the liberal elite because they too felt persecuted at the hands of the liberal elite – at least, to a greater extent than they felt empowered by the example of Hillary Clinton. Less-educated white males, the group on whom contemporary liberal rights confer the least practical benefit, voted by a staggering 49-point margin for Donald Trump. This is the group most susceptible to Hofstadter's paranoid style. Hofstadter wrote of this group in his 1964 essay that "America has been largely taken away from them and their kind" and ridiculed their attempts to repossess it as "the animosities and passions of a small minority." In characterizing nativist whites as a small minority, Hofstadter fell into the classic sociological trap of assuming that most other people are like him (educated, well-traveled, upwardly mobile). Half a century later, relentlessly rising inequality has brought know-nothing nativism back with a vengeance. Trump offered to give these nativists "their" country back. As he promised in his inaugural address: "You will never be ignored again."

Hell hath no fury like a suitor scorned. The hatred that liberal women and the liberal political class feel toward Donald Trump is not the tsk-tsk disapproval of an overly licentious alpha male like Bill Clinton, nor is it the rational disavowal of a policy program like that of George W. Bush. It is the inarticulate anger of a class of experts whose extensive credentials have been rejected in favor of the inchoate promises of a bumptious, boorish billionaire. Hillary Clinton's characterization of Trump supporters as "racist, sexist, homophobic, xenophobic, Islamophobic – you name it" was remarkably reminiscent of Hofstadter's take on the Goldwater nativists of 1964. For a century and a half since the death of Jacksonian Democracy, progressives and conservatives oscillated in power, but the authority of America's expert class has never been seriously challenged. Until now. On election day 2016, Clinton's "basket of deplorables" looked the country's liberals dead in the eye and said: "You're fired."

5

The Populist Purgative

Donald Trump wasn't the only one challenging the authority of the expert class in 2016. In Britain, cabinet minister Michael Gove remarked in the run-up to Brexit that "the people of this country have had enough of experts . . . saying that they know what is best and getting it consistently wrong." He was interrupted at "experts" and a classic quote was born. Bernie Sanders, too, challenged the liberal orthodoxy on issues like government spending, corporate taxes, foreign trade, public education, and universal healthcare. Like Trump, he also defied the pundits in his language and messaging, associating himself with the taboo word "socialist." Had Hillary Clinton stood aside, it is quite likely that Bernie Sanders would have trumped Trump in the general election. It seems shocking to consider that the 2016 election that brought Donald Trump to power was so wide open that the United States just missed out on electing a self-proclaimed socialist to the Oval Office. We might all join Hillary Clinton in asking: what happened?

What happened was that the Democrats and Republicans offered the voters a choice of candidates without offering them a choice of policies. Democracy requires more than just elections. It also requires a choice about what (not just who) to vote for. In Anglo-American politics, that choice has historically been between conservative parties that embrace stability and tradition and progressive parties that advocate redistribution and change. In England those are clearly identifiable as the Conservative Party and the Labour Party; in America they are the Republicans and the Democrats. Anglo-American politics have never been a simple two-sided game: England has a liberal party (the Liberal Democrats) while in the United States both major parties have hosted liberal wings. Nonetheless, Anglo-American elections have historically offered a clear choice between conservative and progressive agendas. The liberals may swing elections, but they don't win them.

The three Anglo-American traditions of conservatism, progressivism, and liberalism interact to make Anglo-American democracy the most successful political system in history. Success is a subjective evaluation, but if we can judge political systems by the degree to which they allow individual human beings to flourish while maintaining the long-term stability of the societies that nourish them, then Anglo-American democracy has been successful indeed. Anglo-American institutions have proven themselves remarkably adaptable while at the same time incredibly robust. Americans still live under a Constitution that came into effect in 1789. The United Kingdom is governed by a constitution so old that it was never written down in the first place. The three-cornered competition of conservatives, progressives, and liberals puts Anglo-American political society on a stable ideological footing. Conservatives and progressives compete to score votes while liberals referee the match.

At least, that's how things were until the liberal ideological victories of the 1960s. Since then there hasn't been much to fight over. Despite increasingly rabid campaign rhetoric, both major parties have embraced a mix of free trade, environmental protection, low taxes on investment, high taxes on salaries, and minimal anti-poverty support that is neither conservative nor progressive but distinctively liberal. Barack Obama pushed through his healthcare reform program without a single Republican vote, after which Congressional Republicans thwarted Donald Trump's efforts to repeal it. Bipartisan cooperation may be dead, but that hardly matters when both parties pursue the same policies when in power. Democrats have been promising to legislate abortion rights for forty years, Republicans to abolish them. They have continued to be governed by the 1973 Supreme Court decision in *Roe v. Wade*.

As a result, many Americans no longer feel like they do live in a democracy, at least where the federal government is concerned. More than half the electorate now believes that the government is not run "for the benefit of all," according to data from the American National Election Studies (ANES). This wasn't always the case. When the ANES were first conducted in the 1960s, a clear majority believed that the government was run in the public interest. Since then, faith in the government has topped 50 percent only once, in the immediate aftermath of the September 11 attacks. The same pattern holds for the ANES question on "trust in the federal government." Notably, Gallup Poll data show that trust in state governments has declined much less, and trust in local governments hasn't declined at all. The time-honored aphorism that "all politics is local" may be turning into reality, but that's not the way it's supposed to be. The major parties are supposed to fight things out at the national level, too.

How can it be that the exclusionary party machine politics of the 1960s inspired more confidence in government than today's clean, civil, closely monitored elections? Until the 1960s, both major political parties selected delegates to their national conventions in closed-door caucuses; Presidential candidates were effectively chosen by consensus among older white rich men in (literally) smoke-filled rooms. Today, most states have open primaries, and those caucuses that remain are now open as well. The parties themselves are also much more open, making it easier for outsiders to run and win (just look at Barack Obama and Donald Trump). Congress is more racially diverse than ever and the number of women in Congress has quintupled since the 1960s, even if minorities and women are still seriously underrepresented. In terms of democratic procedure, it's hard to think of any way in which American democracy has become less robust over the last half century. What happened was not a failure of process. What happened was a failure of substance.

The New Authoritarianism

Populism and the great flood

The notably less liberal democracy of America's old caucus system had one advantage over today's much more inclusive political process: those rich white men of yesteryear tended to offer much clearer policy alternatives, and once in office put their policies into effect. Everyone who voted for Andrew Jackson in 1828 knew that he would get rid of the Second Bank of the United States; everyone who voted for William Jennings Bryan in 1896 knew that, if elected, he would take the country off the gold standard; everyone who voted for Franklin Roosevelt in 1932 knew that he would fight for a "New Deal" for the American people. The opponents of all of these policies called them crazy, even catastrophic, and did everything they could to block them. But the voters were justified in expecting that changes of party meant changes of policy – that "elections have consequences," as Barack Obama so ironically quipped on his fourth day in office. Or as the satirist H.L. Mencken put it in 1915: "Democracy is the theory that the common people know what they want, and deserve to get it good and hard."

Mencken was the journalist who labeled the July 1925 Scopes trial the "Monkey Trial." Later that same month he wrote of William Jennings Bryan, counsel for the prosecution, that he was "a peasant come home to the dung-pile." This, in his obituary. In 1928 he wrote of Andrew Jackson that "No man ever entered the White House under the burden of a more inconvenient past." One can only wonder what he would have made of Donald Trump. Mencken would go on to excoriate Franklin Roosevelt's New Deal as a program that "began, like the Salvation Army, by promising to save humanity ... and ended, again like the Salvation Army, by running flop-houses and disturbing the peace." Jackson, Bryan, and Roosevelt were all reviled in their days by leading intellectuals, however much their reputations (especially Roosevelt's) may have subsequently evolved. All three were wealthy celebrities beloved of the poor and uneducated, and all three were condemned as class traitors by polite society. And all three, of course, were populists.

The election of Andrew Jackson to the Presidency in 1828 swept away the so-called "Era of Good Feelings" during which the young Republic's elite had reached a consensus on most of the major issues of the day. In the previous election (1824) all four major candidates had actually run as members of the same party. Andrew Jackson had won a plurality of both the popular vote and the Electoral College, but since he lacked an absolute majority the decision was passed to the House of Representatives, which selected his arch-rival the former Federalist John Quincy Adams. Jackson had his revenge in the landslide victory of 1828. For a generation in the early nineteenth century, American voters had been offered the consensus politics of a technocratic elite. That consensus had served the country well, firmly establishing American independence (not a sure thing in the early 1800s), formulating an effective foreign policy, and mitigating the boom-and-bust fluctuations of an immature but rapidly growing economy. But it was a consensus.

Functioning democracy requires a choice between competing candidates with competing visions of the future. Without choice, voting is futile. Voting pretty much collapsed in the uncontested election of 1820 at the height of the Era of Good Feelings. It quadrupled between 1824 and the awkward four-way, one-party election of 1824. It tripled again between 1824 and the straightforward choice of Adams versus Jackson in 1828. The more than twelve-fold rise in the vote count over just eight years was partly due to the expansion of the electorate. But most of it was due to the fact that in 1828 elections once again "had consequences." Jackson's platform was radically different from

Adams', and once in office Jackson vigorously pushed it through. Jackson pulled the plug on the Bank of the United States, ushering in an era of inflationary monetary policy and boom-and-bust speculation. He also pursued a policy of aggressive territorial expansion, culminating in the infamous "Trail of Tears" of Native American removals on the southeastern frontier and a war against the Seminole Tribe of Florida. Few experts then or now would defend such policies. But the voters knew what they wanted, and they got it good and hard. Politically excluded Native Americans and African-Americans got it even harder.

William Jennings Bryan never got the chance to push through his policies, but his unsuccessful candidacy at least gave the voters a choice during a period of widespread elite consensus. The sitting Democratic President, Grover Cleveland, was virtually a closet Republican, sharing the Republican commitment to the gold standard. In the populist revolt year of 1896, his renomination was a non-starter. This pattern was repeated with different results in 1932, when populists pushed the radically progressive Franklin Roosevelt to the Democratic nomination over the technocratic, pro-business Hoover clone Al Smith. Smith had unsuccessfully challenged the similarly technocratic, pro-business

Republican Herbert Hoover for the Presidency in 1928. The nomination of Roosevelt as the Democratic Party candidate for President at the low point of the Great Depression gave the voters a clear choice between a hands-off, business-oriented approach to the economy and activist government intervention to raise agricultural prices and create jobs. The jury is still out on who actually had the better program to end the depression. But Roosevelt's candidacy gave people the power to choose, and overwhelmingly they chose Roosevelt.

Populism doesn't well up from some mysterious depth of primordial group solidarity, turning otherwise rational voters into an unthinking mob ripe for exploitation by Nazis, Fascists, and other ne'er-do-wells. Political scientists like Cas Mudde and Jan-Werner Müller say that populists reject the pluralism of contemporary societies. If that were true, every election season would see a wave of majoritarian ignoramuses rallying together to march to inevitable triumph. In reality, populism is a strategy of desperation, pursued by people whose policy preferences have been excluded from the political debate – and the populists usually lose. Populism is a last-gasp strategy for breaking through the expert consensus on the universe of sound policy options, a strategy for challenging the authority of experts to determine the boundaries of legitimate political discourse. Populism arises as a response to the rhetorical dominance of liberal intellectuals in polite political society. Populists are the hooligans who boo the seemingly biased liberal referee.

The great spiritual danger facing twenty-first-century democracy is that liberal intellectuals increasingly dismiss the moral right of less-educated people to have opinions that conflict with the consensus wisdom of the expert class. Functioning democracy requires that the most exalted experts engage seriously with the mundane views of ordinary citizens. Populism is a way to make sure that they do. It forces the political class to respect the dignity of the electorate. Trump was widely ridiculed for saying "I love the poorly educated"; he had the last laugh when they voted for him. The democratic principle of one person, one vote is a tonic for humility because it requires politicians to suspend their preconceptions about the intellectual incapacity of ordinary people. British Prime Minister Gordon Brown didn't understand that when he called one of his supporters a "bigoted woman" for recounting her fears about immigration. Hillary Clinton certainly didn't get it when she candidly called nearly half of the American population a "basket of deplorables." Donald Trump, the least humble politician of all, got it. And it got him the Presidency.

Populism is the Biblical flood that has the potential to wash away a dysfunctional party system and its sterile political covenants. It is up to the survivors of that flood to rebuild a better political home for the people and their representatives. The "Trump effect" may jolt the Republican Party into reinventing itself as a stronger, more effective, more representative party once he leaves office. The "Sanders effect" almost did just that for the Democrats in 2016, though the liberal Democratic Party establishment fought back hard to retain control. Notice how the British political system sprung back into shape just one year after the populist purgative of Brexit: the 2017 general election may have proved inconclusive in Parliamentary terms, but the combined vote of the two major parties shot up from 67 percent to 82 percent, the highest level since Britain joined the European Economic Community (precursor to the European Union) in 1973. British voters abandoned boutique parties in droves as soon as the two major parties returned to pre-EU politics as usual. With luck, the slower-moving American political system may follow suit in 2020 or 2024. For liberals, that will be a long time to wait. For everyone else, politics has suddenly regained its relevance.

From Gettysburg to Charlottesville

In his Gettysburg Address of November 19, 1863, Abraham Lincoln offered perhaps the most dignified definition of democracy ever pronounced. Speaking at the consecration of the Gettysburg National Cemetery, with the Civil War still undecided, he called on the great and the good of the war-torn country's political elite assembled on the late battlefield to resolve "that government of the people, by the people, for the people, shall not perish from the earth." Everyone knows Lincoln's words; few people know their source. Lincoln was roughly quoting from the American Unitarian minister Theodore Parker. In an 1850 speech to the New England Anti-Slavery Convention, Parker argued that the "American idea" of freedom, as reflected in the US Declaration of Independence, "demands, as the proximate organization thereof, a democracy, that is, a government of all the people, by all the people, for all the people."

Parker's original makes clear the intention of those otherwise ambiguous prepositions of, by, and for. For the abolitionist Parker, the realization of a government of all the people, by all the people, for all the people was only possible in a country without slavery. Parker condemned slavery as creating in America "an aristocracy, that is, a government of all the people by a part of the people . . . for a part of the people." In Parker's analysis, this sowed the seeds of a permanent conflict from which neither the master nor the slave could ever break free until the institution of slavery itself was abolished. For Parker the specifically "American" resolution to the master–slave dialectic was democracy. Parker had read his Hegel. In his posthumously published *Lectures on the Philosophy of History*, the German philosopher Georg Hegel had proclaimed that "the History of the World is nothing but the development of the idea of Freedom." Parker's "American idea" of freedom was universal suffrage under the equal protection of the law.

Lincoln may not have read Hegel, but he is known to have read Parker. Parker was a celebrity Boston preacher whose parishioners included a who's who of the abolitionist movement, including Julia Ward Howe (author of the "Battle Hymn of the Republic"). Parker's 1850 New England speech was widely known and quoted at the time. It was also reprinted in an 1863 edition of Parker's speeches collected under the title *Discourses of Slavery*, published in London just months before Lincoln's Gettysburg Address. It is quite possible that the new book, hot off the presses, was making the rounds in Washington when Lincoln was drafting his text. If so, he may have been inspired directly by the words of Parker's speech, a passionate argument for the abolition of slavery and the preservation of the union. Speculation aside, experts agree that Lincoln was aware of Parker's definition of democracy and used it as the basis for his remarks.

Fulfilling the terrible prophecy of the Battle Hymn, Lincoln did "die to make men free," but not before ensuring for the whole United States a single government of all the people, Northerners and Southerners alike. It took another century, but the liberal reforms of the 1960s finally fulfilled the Great Emancipator's promise of government by all the people, white and black alike. Government for all the people is another matter.

Ensuring government for all the people has historically been the mission of the Democratic Party. For a century and a half from Andrew Jackson to Lyndon Johnson the Democratic Party stood for activist government in the interest of the "common man." As the Democratic hero William Jennings Bryan put it in the Cross of Gold speech:

> There are two ideas of government. There are those who believe that if you just legislate to make the well-to-do prosperous, that their prosperity will leak through on those below. The Democratic idea has been that if you legislate to make the masses prosperous their prosperity will find its way up and through every class that rests upon it.

Meanwhile Republicans, usually acting in alliance with the country's liberal business elite, countered with sound money and balanced budgets. Recent Republican Presidents may have run big deficits, but certainly not in the interest of the "common man." They ran up deficits by cutting taxes in a vain attempt to "starve the beast" of government spending, as the memorable Republican mantra puts it. The beast has proven remarkably resilient.

Until 1970 the Republican Party hosted a robust liberal wing that kept the party in line on deficit spending. But when the arch-conservative Richard Nixon embraced the openly racist "Southern Strategy" to bring the states of the Old Confederacy into the Republican camp, liberals abandoned the party in droves. By the 1980s the words "liberal" and Democrat" had become synonymous in most people's minds, causing endless linguistic confusion. In reality, the liberals haven't changed; they've just changed their party. Before 1970, most American liberals were to be found in the Republican Party, though they were present in substantial numbers in the Democratic Party as well. After 1970, liberals came to be so overwhelmingly concentrated in the Democratic Party that they took control of the party outright. For a while that made the Democratic Party the "natural party of government" – though Republicans have been remarkably effective at preventing Democrats from translating the liberal–progressive alliance into electoral success.

Though relatively small in absolute number, the liberal intelligentsia forms a wildly disproportionate segment of the political class. Professionals of the pen like lawyers, journalists, and academics all tend toward liberalism. The liberal takeover of the Democratic Party put them in charge of a major American political party for the first time since the demise of the old Federalists at the dawn of the republic. That must be gratifying for liberals, but it may not be good for the liberal cause. Back when both major parties had liberal wings, liberals were in a position to continuously moderate the extremes of American political discourse, thereby improving the quality of political debate (and policy-making) no matter who was in power. For a century from Reconstruction to the civil rights era liberals were central to the construction of bipartisan coalitions that pushed forward the business of government. But now that the cause of liberalism is tied to the fate of one party, the ability of liberals to communicate across party lines has collapsed.

Their ability to communicate with the less-educated majority of society has also been compromised. Only about one-third of the US population has a university education, and one-eighth a postgraduate degree. Clinton won those groups by 5 points and 21 points, respectively. But "the people," as Democratic icons like Roosevelt and Bryan would have understood the term, ordinary workers without advanced degrees, are no longer a core constituency of the Democratic Party. Nor have they ever been a core constituency of the Republican Party. Excluded from the policy counsels of both parties, they have become the great wildcard of American politics: the "Reagan Democrats," the "Tea Party," and the "deplorables" who voted for Donald Trump. Unable to keep them in the party, and perhaps embarrassed by their often illiberal demands, today's Democratic Party establishment has been working hard to drive them out of politics altogether. Witness the Confederate Monuments removal movement.

Today's Democratic Party has come to celebrate

minority identities to the point where it eagerly anticipates a future in which it believes the United States will become a majority-minority country; this is a cheerfully multicultural but politically sterile dream, if the only thing those minorities have in common with each other is their lack of a common identity. Meanwhile the Republican Party has descended into a similarly sterile conservative obstructionism whose highest purpose is, as their patron saint Ronald Reagan so famously made clear, to prevent the government from trying to improve people's lives: "The nine most terrifying words in the English language are 'I'm from the government, and I'm here to help.'" Neither position is intrinsically at odds with the free and fair electoral processes that ensure government by (all) the people. Both positions undermine the chances of any kind of government that genuinely works for (all) the people. Donald Trump seems unlikely to do any better, but the populist revolt that brought him to office has the potential to prod (or more likely, to scare) the country's entire political establishment into respecting the dignity of (all) the people the next time around.

The New Authoritarianism

The best form of government

Political pundits of all stripes are fond of quoting Winston Churchill's famous dictum that "it has been said that democracy is the worst form of government except all those other forms that have been tried from time to time." Perhaps they should consider the alternative: that democracy is in fact the best possible form of government, an institution to be loved and cherished. Thomas Jefferson surely thought so. So did Abraham Lincoln. And if you read his full speech, so too did Winston Churchill. Put back in context, Churchill's famous maxim continues: "but there is the broad feeling in our country that the people should rule, continuously rule, and that public opinion, expressed by all constitutional means, should shape, guide, and control the actions of Ministers who are their servants and not their masters." For Churchill, democracy wasn't just "not bad." It was absolutely good.

The passage is drawn from the 1947 debate on the Labour Party's Parliament Bill, which Churchill opposed on the grounds that it would dilute the people's ability to hold Parliament accountable to their will. The Bill, ultimately passed into law over the opposition of the House of Lords, reduced the Lords' ability to delay legislation originating in the

House of Commons. In his speech opposing the Bill, Churchill made frequent reference to American democracy, even quoting Lincoln's definition of democracy as the government "of the people, by the people, for the people." Churchill admired the US Constitution, which in his appraisal "embodied much of the ancient wisdom of this island," and firmly believed in the value of its "checks and counterchecks." But he also admired its "frequent appeals to the people."

Despite his opposition to the Labour government of the day, in his speech Churchill went on to acknowledge that there is

> a difference between the two sides in our political life. Temperament, conditions, upbringing, fortunes, interests, environment decide for every individual in a free country which side he will take. One side claims to be the party of progress, as if progress was bound to be right, no matter in what direction. The other side emphasises stability, which is also very important in this changing world.

Churchill argued that the tension between these two sides, between progress and stability, was the essence of good government. "Both progress and stability are needed to make a happy country." A more eloquent description of the basic alignment of the Anglo-American political system cannot be found.

It is ironic that Churchill failed to credit the other great Anglo-American political tradition, liberalism. Ironic, because Churchill first achieved national acclaim as a cabinet minister for the Liberal Party. Perhaps it was an oversight. Perhaps it was because by 1947 the Liberal Party was a spent force. In his remarks that day Churchill reminisced fondly on his Liberal past, but said nothing of the liberal present. Maybe for him liberalism had achieved all it had set out to do, and was no longer needed.

But in a 1908 speech on "Liberalism and Socialism" in which he considered all three of the great Anglo-American political traditions, a much younger Churchill had appealed for the preservation of liberalism:

> Don't think that Liberalism is a faith that is played out; that it is a philosophy to which there is no expanding future. As long as the world rolls round Liberalism will have its part to play – a grand, beneficent, and ameliorating part to play – in relation to men and States.

He continued with the defiant pledge that "Liberalism will not be killed." Of course, it was killed, at least as a governing political party in the

United Kingdom. It lived on as a force that permeates the whole party system, sometimes undermining it but more often strengthening it. And it is just as vital in the United States as in the United Kingdom. All three political traditions, liberalism included, are indispensable to the health of Anglo-American democracy. As Churchill pleaded at the end of his 1908 speech, echoing the Gospel of Saint John:

> Let us build wisely, let us build surely, let us build faithfully, let us build not for the moment, but for the years that are to come, and so establish here below what we hope to find above – a house of many mansions, where there shall be room for all.